TICKET TO TOLTEC

A MILE BY MILE GUIDE
for the
Cumbres & Toltec
Scenic Railroad

by

Doris B. Osterwald

Doris B. Osterwald
author of

CINDERS & SMOKE

*A mile by mile guide for the
Durango to Silverton narrow gauge trip*

and

NARROW GAUGE TO CUMBRES

A Pictorial History of the Cumbres and Toltec Scenic Railroad

WESTERN GUIDEWAYS
P. O. Box 15532
Lakewood, Colorado 80215

$4.00

First Edition

Copyright 1976

by

Doris B. Osterwald

All rights reserved.

Printed by:

Metzger Printing and Publishing Co.
Denver, Colorado

This book is dedicated
to my husband Frank,
with love and thanks.

ACKNOWLEDGEMENTS

When the last corrections have been made and all the commas put in their proper places (I hope), and the printer has taken over, a flood of memories engulf the writer. So many friends and associates have helped in so many ways, a simple thank you for their efforts on my behalf seems inadequate. Most of all, my family have been patient when Ma was busy at the typewriter, drafting table, or library. All have made invaluable contributions; my heartfelt thanks. We had many great days riding and watching C&TS trains. Candy Wood and Ed Osterwald field-checked the geologic maps.

W. D. Freeman of Sidney, Australia reviewed the manuscript critically and technically. His meticulous notes and suggestions for improving the accuracy and clarity have been invaluable. Thank you, Bill. Jackson C. Thode, of the D&RGW Railroad, was most helpful in identifying old photographs and also supplied much technical data on construction of the San Juan Extension, and on the bridges, buildings, snowsheds, historical facts, and photographs. Alexis McKinney, formerly with the Rio Grande, arranged for me to obtain a complete set of engineering drawings of the right of way and track maps for the line, and other historical maps. Robert W. Richardson, of the Colorado Railroad Museum, read the completed manuscript for accuracy and made many suggestions for improvement. Gordon Chappell showed me many historic points of interest as we rode the "Toltec Rattler."

Many individuals were most generous in sharing their photographs. A very special thank you to W. D. Joyce of Antonito, Colorado for the many fine photographs and hours spent in sharing his memories of the Rio Grande in the early 1900's. Turner Van Nort, of Oklahoma City, Oklahoma, generously donated a number of his photos taken during the 1930's and 1940's. Edna Sanborn, Ray Jones, Jim Shawcroft, Kenneth Flansburg, Ernest Robart, Gordon Chappell and the late Trudy Hollenbeck also contributed photographs.

The staff of the State Historical Society of Colorado and the Denver Public Library, Western History Department, helped track down old photos and unearth little-known facts about the San Juan Extension.

Background information on railroad operation and history was generously given by Ben Greathouse, retired D&RGW Engineer, the late Ed Romero of Chama, Don Graham also of Chama, Castellar Garcia, and Norma and Bud Griffin of Antonito, Colorado.

Employees and officials of the Cumbres & Toltec Scenic Railroad who were most helpful in sharing information include John Oldberg, Fritz Bauer, Gary Getman, John Coker, Ross Osborne, and Gary Breeding.

Mrs. Phillip Gallegos of Chama graciously translated some old Spanish records, Jo Doubek deciphered my handwriting and typed the final manuscript, Susan Schmitt helped immeasurably with the final cover design, and Ellen Hansen with drafting problems. My dear friend, Polly Stanley, arrived from Evanston, Ill. in time to help with reading proof.

Finally, a very special thank you to all the staff of Metzger Printing and Publishing Co., a really great group of people to work with.

CONTENTS

Cover photograph—East Entrance Toltec Tunnel (Ed Osterwald)

Back cover—West Entrance Toltec Tunnel and Garfield Monument (F. W. Osterwald)

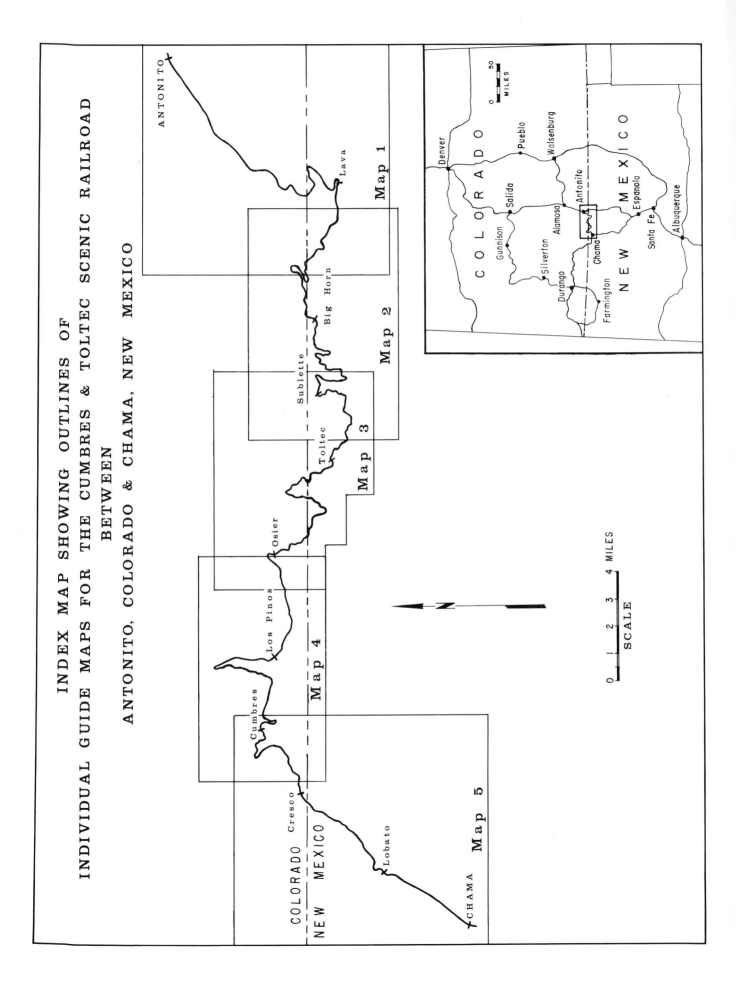

INDEX MAP SHOWING OUTLINES OF
INDIVIDUAL GUIDE MAPS FOR THE CUMBRES & TOLTEC SCENIC RAILROAD
BETWEEN
ANTONITO, COLORADO & CHAMA, NEW MEXICO

-6-

INTRODUCTION

Welcome aboard the CUMBRES AND TOLTEC SCENIC RAILROAD. You are about to leave on an unforgettable trip on one of the few railroads in the United States that carries passengers in converted freight cars pulled by steam locomotives! These cars formerly were used to carry supplies and equipment to mines in the San Juan Mountains, and ore concentrates out of the mountains to the smelters. Nowhere else in the country can you experience the thrill of seeing a remote, and virtually unspoiled area from an open gondola that once carried coal.

So let's step back into the nineteenth century for a day, and enjoy the scenery and train trip as earlier tourists did, even though we are not in a fancy passenger train operated by the Denver and Rio Grande Railway Co. One such train was described in the March 31, 1881 issue of the Pueblo, Colorado **Weekly Colorado Chieftan:**

> "A complete passenger train consisting of an express, baggage, mail car, two coaches, and two pullman sleepers passed through this city yesterday afternoon for the San Juan Division, and will be put into service on that division when the new timetable takes effect."

In later years **the** way to travel to Durango was on the plush "San Juan" passenger train.

This book is an attempt to combine an explanation of the scenic beauty and geology visible from the train, with the history of the area and of the construction of the D&RG San Juan Extension.

EARLY RAILROAD HISTORY

The Denver and Rio Grande Railway Company was granted a charter in October, 1870 to build a railroad from Denver, south to El Paso, Texas. The company also planned to extend rails into Mexico. The planned route to El Paso was south to Pueblo, west through the Arkansas River Canyon (Royal Gorge), across Poncha Pass (then called Poncho Pass), and into the San Luis Valley to the Rio Grande. There, tracks were to follow the river south to El Paso. Six branches were planned to the mining areas of Colorado and one branch was projected to reach Salt Lake City, Utah.

One year later, trains were operating between Denver and Colorado Springs. Construction continued and Pueblo was reached in 1872. Money problems delayed construction for several years, however, and track did not reach La Veta, Colorado until 1876. By that time, mining activity in central and southwestern Colorado was booming, a fact which caused the D&RG to forget El Paso, and turn west toward the irresistable lure of mining riches. In 1877 rails were completed to El Moro, near Trinidad, and across Veta Pass to Garland City (now Ft. Garland) in the San Luis Valley. In July of 1978 narrow gauge track lay beside the cottonwood trees along the Rio Grande River at the new company town of Alamosa. Thus 8 years after its inception, the D&RG Railway could justify its name.

Financial problems continued to haunt the railroad, however, and an expensive court fight with the Atchison, Topeka and Santa Fe Railroad over rights-of-way in Raton Pass and Royal Gorge, stopped all construction until the suit was settled by a U. S. Supreme Court decision on April 21, 1879. A final settlement between the two railroads was signed in Boston, Mass. on March 27, 1880. The terms stipulated that the D&RG could not build south of Espanola, N.M. for 10 years, and that the AT&SF was forbidden to construct any more track westward toward Leadville via the Royal Gorge.

When the Rio Grande realized they had finally won the route to Leadville and other Colorado mining towns, new money for construction appeared. In August, 1879, the D&RG announced that it would begin immediately to build a branch to the San Juans and another branch south to Espanola, N.M. Contracts were let in December, 1879, for track to be laid south of Alamosa on a grade that had been built two years before. Track laying started in February, 1880 and by the end of March, the wobbly 40-pound steel rails reached the new "town" of Antonito. Early newspaper articles referred to this town as San Antonio, but in the 1880 annual report for the railroad, it was called Antonito. From Antonito the railroad divided, one track going southward past Tres Piedras, N.M. to Espanola, N.M., and the track for the San Juan Extension going southwestward toward the mountains.

Now the westward plunge into the mountains started. Why was the route over Cumbres Pass chosen by the D&RG locating engineers? To quote from the Annual Report of the railroad for 1880:

> ". . . Our engineering parties had been examining the mountain range dividing the waters of the Rio Grande from the waters of the San Juan, with a view of securing the best line to the town of Silverton, in the heart of the San Juan mining country.
>
> Lines were run over Cunningham Pass, South Fork Pass, and Alamosa Pass, and barometric examinations made of other parts of the range, and late in the summer of 1879 the route along which we are now constructing was adopted."

The Cumbres Pass route appears to have been a compromise. Although it was not nearly as high as Cunningham Pass, and thus less difficult to build and maintain, it was much longer. (Probably no records were available at that time of the depth of winter snows on Cumbres!) Also, the Parkview and Conejos Toll Road was open and offered an easy way to transport grading crews and equipment, as the projected railroad followed the toll road in a general way. The easily accessible coal deposits west of Chama may have been another reason this route was selected, in addition to the distinct possibility that the AT&SF might build a line to the San Juans from the south. It was thought that the Cumbres Pass route would forestall any such construction by the Santa Fe.

The D&RG decided in 1870 to build its railroad "narrow gauge" (rails 3 feet apart) rather than "standard guage" (4 feet 8½ inches wide) which was used on most other railroads. The choice was made because narrow gauge construction was cheaper, equipment cost less, and sharper curves were possible. Thus it was better adapted to mountainous terrain. The railroad was only 11 years old, however, when the management realized they were bucking great odds with a narrow gauge operation. Consequently, by late 1890, the main line to Salt Lake City was standard gauged. Some portions of the narrow gauge in Colorado and New Mexico managed to survive until the 1940's and

1950's. Of these routes, only the D&RGW's Silverton Branch showed a profit by the early 1960's, when tourists discovered the pleasure of a leisurely journey along the Animas River to Silverton. Although the Cumbres Pass route was used frequently, passenger service ceased in January 1951. Finally in September, 1967, the D&RGW requested permission to abandon the line from Antonito to Durango, and Farmington, N.M.

By 1968 many individuals and organizations started to consider seriously the possibility of preserving at least a portion of the San Juan Extension for use as a tourist line. After much discussion, the states of Colorado and New Mexico joined forces, and through legislative actions each state created a Railroad Authority. Thus, the New Mexico and Colorado Railroad Authorities were able to purchase 64 miles of track between Chama and Antonito for $547,120.00 in July 1970. The track from Chama to Durango and Farmington, N.M. was scrapped. Final terms between the Rio Grande and the states were completed by July, and on September 1, the first of three large shipments of engines, rolling stock, and non-revenue equipment were delivered in Antonito to the Cumbres & Toltec Scenic Railroad. The fall of 1970 was a busy time for many persons who volunteered to aid in moving the engines and rolling stock to Chama for winter storage, as Antonito had no available storage track or yards.

The C&TS actually is owned by the citizens of Colorado and New Mexico, who control and finance it through the two Railroad Authorities. In 1971, the Colorado-New Mexico Railroad Authorities, acting jointly, granted a lease to Scenic Railways, Inc. of Los Altos, California to operate the line for the first season. In 1972, the firm was granted a 20-year lease for continued operation. Because it is an interstate common carrier, the C&TS also is subject to inspection and regulation by the Interstate Commerce Commission, as well as by various agencies of the two states. Recently the C&TS became a Registered National Historic Site.

The first public excursion of the Cumbres & Toltec Scenic Railroad was on June 26, 1971, and since that time, about 100,000 people have had the pleasure of seeing Toltec Gorge, eating lunch at Osier, drifting along the Rio de los Pinos, and looking down into the Chama Valley from spectacular Windy Point.

HOW THE TRAIN WORKS

Steam engines have become rare. Although most people know that coal and water go into the tender, for use in the engine, some may not know how these materials are converted into power to pull the train. Coal is burned in a fire-box in the engine cab, very similar to an old fashioned coal furnace. Heat from the fire passes through many tubes (called flues) in the boiler, which is the part of the engine ahead of the fire-box. The tubes are surrounded by water. The water is heated and converted into steam, which is fed through valves to two cylinders, one on each side of the engine, ahead of the drive wheels. These cylinders, which are very much like the cylinders in an automobile, each contain a movable piston that is connected to the main rods which pivot on the drive wheels. Steam expands in the front of one cylinder, driving the piston and main rod backward, and also

expands in the rear of the other cylinder driving that piston and rod forward. This backward and forward motion of the rods causes the wheels to turn. Motion of the wheels reverses the motion of the rods and pistons, forcing spent steam out of the cylinders and up the stack. This exhausted steam makes the choo-choo-choo sound that is so characteristic of steam locomotives—four choo sounds (exhausts) for each turn of the drive wheels.

On the left side of the engine is a contraption made up of small tanks and pipes that usually leaks a little steam. When the train is stopped this contraption makes a characteristic ka-thunk—ka-thunk sound. This device is an air compressor, driven by steam from the boiler, which provides air pressure to operate the brakes on the entire train. Beneath the couplers on each car and on the engine are large rubber hoses. These hoses are connected to form a continuous air line from the engine to the rear of the train. The brakes, however, operate differently from the brakes on your car, which are applied by increasing the pressure in the system when you press the brake pedal. About 70 to 90 pounds per square inch air pressure is maintained in the air line when the train is moving. When the engineer operates his brake lever, air pressure in the line is reduced, causing cylinders on each car to force the brake shoes against the wheels, thus slowing the train. The conductor can also "pull the air" from the rear of the train in an emergency. For safety in descending steep hills, "retainers" on the cars can be set to hold lower air pressures, allowing the brakes to drag slightly (see photo, p. 81). If the air line is opened anywhere, the brakes will "go into emergency" and stop the train, until the line is again closed and pressure allowed to build up. Large steel handwheels sticking above the roof on one end of each car are used to lock the brakes by hand when cars are stored, much like the parking brake in your car. Air brakes are nothing new to the Cumbres Pass narrow gauge. Westinghouse "straight" air brakes were installed on D&RG equipment in 1872; the Rio Grande then became the first U. S. railroad to have air brakes on freight equipment. The "straight" air brakes, however, operated by increasing rather than reducing the air pressure.

Steam-driven cross-compound air pump on left side of C&TS engine 489. Large tank in upper left is a compressed air reservoir. The bank of pipes cools the air after it leaves the pump and before it goes to the reservoir. (C. R. Osterwald)

GUIDE MAPS AND ACCOMPANYING TEXT

This mile by mile guide is written so that points of interest, wreck locations, geology, historic facts, and scenic highlights are keyed to the mileposts set along the track. In some locations, these are the original wooden posts placed in the ground during construction of the San Juan Extension. The wooden posts are about 12 inches square and painted white; a few have been replaced with metal posts. The numbers indicate the distance by rail from Denver where the D&RG started in 1870. Thus, the old stone depot at Antonito is 280.3 miles from Denver because milepost 281 is 0.7 miles westward along the track from the depot. The new C&TS depot is at milepost 280.7.

The five accompanying guide maps graphically show the wooden mileposts. Cross-ties are 1/10 miles apart to aid in following the map with the text. The guide is written so points of interest are described in relation to compass directions. Locations either in front, or behind the train, are given first for the westbound trip from Antonito, and the directions in brackets (   ) represent that for the eastbound trip from Chama. Map symbols used are on page 9. A separate guide, page 45, with 5 geologic maps, explains the geology along the route.

There is also a general guide for the bus or automobile trip between Chama and Antonito on page 39.

Before we leave this morning, the conductor will explain the safety regulations that will be strictly enforced. Please listen; don't let an accident spoil your trip! As the day progresses, the beauty of this remote part of western America will become more apparent to each passenger, and hopefully, no one will be careless and cause a forest fire. The barren hillsides around Osier are the result of a large forest fire in 1879. Do not throw anything out of the cars; trash cans are provided in each car.

On the inside back cover is a list of commonly used whistle signals. With just a little practice, it is easy to interpret the engineer's language as the shrill whistle echoes off the cliffs of nearby canyons.

There is no need to buckle up a seat belt for a flying trip through the vastness of this mountain country. We may approach a speed of as much as 18 miles per hour, but mostly we'll travel at 10 to 12 miles per hour, allowing plenty of time to enjoy every new scene and photograph all the spectacular locations. Have a great day!

EXPLANATION   OF   SYMBOLS

C&TS narrow gauge track. Cross-ties 1/10 mile apart. Milepost—indicates the distance by rail from Denver, Colo.

Tunnel and siding.

Abandoned D&RGW n.g. track.

Water tank or plug.

Snow fences.

Phone booth, station, or section house site.

Railroad station.

Train wreck site.

Garfield Monument.

Abandoned toll road route.

Paved highway.

Dirt road.

C.G.   Campground.

Small communities or homes.

Church.

Rivers and tributary streams.

Cañon   Irrigation ditch.

el. 9,469'   Mountain peak.

State boundary.

County and National Forest boundary.

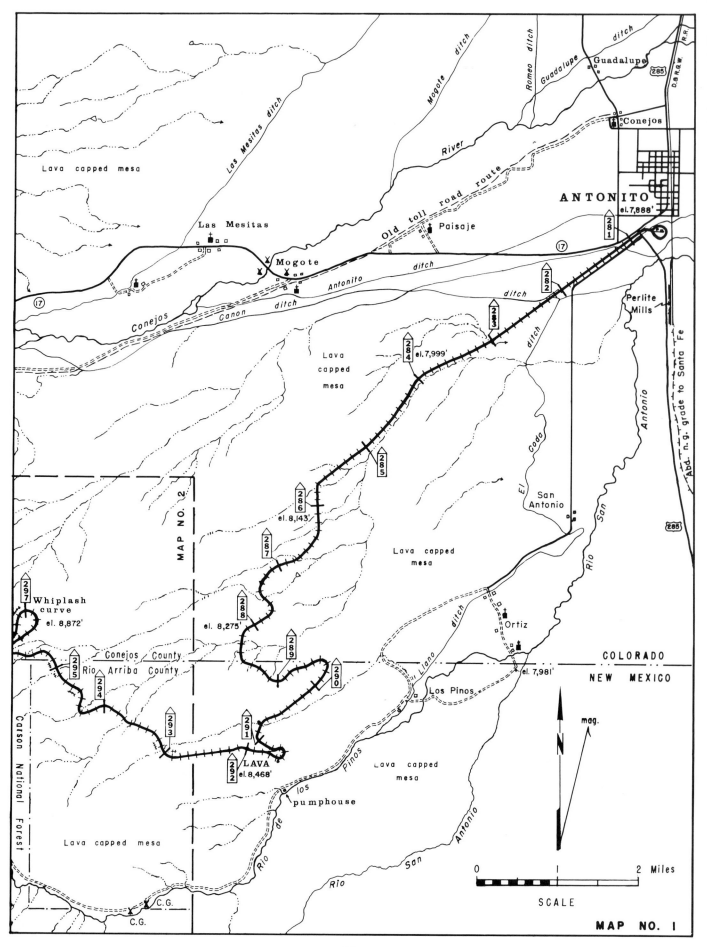

Milepost No. 280.70 ANTONITO, COLORADO, el. 7,888 feet. Eastern terminus of the Cumbres and Toltec Scenic Railroad. Antonito came into being as a railroad town when the first tracks reached the newly platted town on March 31, 1880. It might never have come into existence, if the D&RG Railway had not been determined to reach the mining camps of the San Juan Mountains. Railroad profits were made by land speculation and development, as much as by carrying passengers and freight. Laying out a new town, selling lots, and then bringing newcomers and their needed supplies to the new settlement were more important than attempting to serve an established community. So Conejos, one of the oldest towns in the San Luis Valley, watched as people flocked to the new town.

San Antonio or Antonito was the supply point for the two extensions that were started soon after the rails reached the new town. A depot was finished in April, 1880, and several wooden buildings were under construction. The stone depot was completed later. A large number of tents were also scattered around to house workers and new businesses. One early reporter said that "Antonito is covered with blocks of steel rails, bolts, bars, etc., waiting to be used at the front." Estimates of the amount of rail on hand varied from 60 to 75 miles.

For hundreds of years previously, the San Luis Valley had been home to the Ute Indians. Beginning in the 1840's the first Spanish-speaking people from New Mexico began to venture into the valley to establish farms and ranches. Many battles with the Indians were fought before the proud Utes signed a treaty that "gave" their land to the white man. The Spanish influence is very apparent in Antonito, Conejos and other communities in the valley. These hard-working farmers and ranchers love the land, as did the Indians, and they have left an indelible mark on it with their architecture, churches, and life style. A visit to Conejos and surrounding communities is certainly worthwhile.

As the train slowly pulls away from the depot, with plumes of black coal smoke billowing up into the sky, wide, sweeping vistas of distant mountain peaks offer a sneak preview of scenes to come as the day progresses.

Milepost No. 280.86 Cross U.S. Highway 285. Between M.P. 280.90 and M.P. 283.00, is one of three locations on the C&TS route where the track is actually straight! As the journey unfolds, the novelty of this will become apparent.

Milepost No. 281.20 Track crosses Cañon Irrigation Ditch. The oldest irrigation projects in Colorado are near Antonito, with many ditches bringing water from the mountains into the valley to irrigate crops and pastures (Guide Map No. 1). The first trench was dug by hand in 1852, near present day San Luis.

Milepost No. 283.00 Track is on the flat valley floor. The vegetation here is typical of the semi-arid west. Much sagebrush, rabbitbrush, and a number of native grasses grow here with little available water, and a wide variety of wildflowers bloom when sufficient mosture is present.

Purple bee plant blooms here in summer, as does clover and cream-colored stickweed. In the fall, the purple asters (composites) are a delight to see.

Milepost No. 283.06 Cross an 18-foot, 1-panel pile trestle over a small drainage.

Milepost No. 284.79 Cross a 2-panel pile trestle, 28 feet long.

Milepost No. 285.00 Just east of the milepost, a prairie dog town is on the south side of the track. Jackrabbits are plentiful, and occasionally the train will scare up a deer. Gophers also inhabit the area; they are very fond of making a home in the railroad grade, where the digging is easier.

Milepost No. 285.43 Cross a 42-foot bridge over a dry (usually) stream channel.

Milepost No. 285.87 Cross a large bridge over an intermittent stream channel. This is an 80-foot, 5-panel frame trestle.

Milepost No. 286.72 Cross another bridge, a standard 2-panel pile trestle, 28 feet long. On both sides of the track are large gray-green shrubs with dark bark, that shreds in long strips. This is big sagebrush or wormwood, **Artemisia tridentata**, an important plant in the west. It is a valuable food for antelope, elk, and mule deer, because the plant has a high fat content. It provides good ground cover for many small animals and birds. Indians and pioneers pounded the dried seeds into a meal called "pinole." Tea, made from dried sagebrush leaves, has been used as a remedy for colds, for sore eyes, and for hair tonic. Early settlers knew that the land was good for farming if the sagebrush was tall and lush.

Milepost No. 287.00 Cross a cattleguard, just west of the milepost.

Milepost No. 287.49 Cross another bridge, 28 feet long. The first formal excursion over this portion of the San Juan Extension was on October 4-5, 1880 for a group of editors and their wives from Denver, Colorado Springs, and other towns throughout the state. Mr. F. C. Nims, General Passenger Agent for the D&RG was in charge of the arrangements. The train consisted of a Pullman sleeper, chair car, and baggage car. (No mention is made of the engine used on this trip!) Among the guests were William H. Jackson, famous western photographer, and his wife. Soon after this trip, Jackson started to work for the Rio Grande and other western railroads as their publicity photographer. A quote from a long article in the Pueblo, Colorado **Weekly Colorado Chieftain** very graphically describes this first passenger excursion and the country west of Antonito.

"I wish that all whose pulses thrill at the sight of nature's beauties, might have been on the train with us that glorious afternoon. At first we glide smoothly across the plain toward a mesa that seems but a step for a giant; yet our train creeps up its side in a long zig-zag. The cuttings show the underlying rock to be a lava; and we look more reverently upon the cold white peaks in the distance, at the thought that once smoke and ashes belched from their summits, and the fiery streams stained the snow upon their sides."

Milepost No. 288.29 Cross a 3-panel pile trestle, 42 feet long. To the west, the track begins to climb from the flat valley floor onto the mesa (descends from the mesa). The elevation is 8,300 feet above sea level.

Milepost No. 288.55 Cross Colorado-New Mexico state boundary for the first (last) time.

Milepost No. 289.00 To the north, the state boundary is very easy to see! Nice view to the northwest of twin-peaked Los Mogotes, el. 9,818 feet. Los Mogotes means "hummocks" in Spanish. Los Mogotes is a small volcano from which basalt poured onto the surface between 4 and 5 million years ago. On early maps this mountain was called Prospect Peak.

Milepost No. 289.48 Cross Colorado-New Mexico state boundary, and again at 289.71. The boundary between the two states (then U. S. Territories) was first surveyed in 1868, supposedly on the 37th parallel. Later, surveying errors were found, and in 1902-3 a re-survey was authorized by Congress. This re-survey would have reduced the size of Colorado considerably. Arguments between the two states continued until 1925 when the U. S. Supreme Court ruled that the boundary between the two states was that of the very first survey in 1868. The line has since been re-surveyed and portions have been moved about 1200 feet southward, near Cresco, Colorado.

Milepost No. 289.70 East end of long hairpin curve on top of mesa.

Milepost No. 290.77 Lava phone booth was on the north side of the track until about 1973. A 1,084-foot siding at **LAVA** was removed in 1925. Land on both sides of the track is used for livestock grazing.

Milepost No. 291.00 Between M.P. 291.00 and M.P. 292.00 is **LAVA LOOP.** The track makes another tight hairpin curve which is connected by an 826-foot section of track (see Guide Map No. 1). This connection between the main parts of the loop was built some years after the San Juan Extension was completed. Its main purpose was to turn snowplow trains. A U.S.G.S. bench mark at the milepost is 8,479 feet.

Milepost No. 291.55 **LAVA TANK,** el. 8,500 feet. In slightly less than 11 miles from Antonito, the railroad has gained about 600 feet in altitude, rising roughly 50 feet per mile. A correspondent for the Silverton **La Plata Miner** reported in the October 16, 1880 issue that:

> "The second station which has been located just as the first appreciable rise towards the mountains is reached, boasting now of but two buildings, but which may yet become a thrifty burg, is simply a water station."

His next sentence describes Sublette, so the reference must have been of Lava Tank. Today it could hardly be classed as even a "thrifty burg," but the view from here is spectacular. Lava is still "simply a water station." Los Mogotes to the north-northwest is 8 miles away; the high, pyramid-shaped peak on the northeast skyline is Mt. Blanca, el. 14,317 feet, 54 miles distant. The Sangre de Christo range is on the eastern skyline about 32 miles away. The low-lying mountains to the east and northeast of Antonito, called the San Luis Hills, are about 18 miles away. To the south, the round, dome-shaped mountain is an extinct volcano named San Antonio Peak, el. 10,908 feet, 9 miles away. Bighorn Peak is about 5 airline miles distant to the west, but is 8 miles away by rail. The low-lying San Luis Valley to the east and north is part of the Rio Grande Trough (see Geology, p. 45).

The original tank at **LAVA** was burned in the fall of 1971, probably by a careless photographer who had climbed to the top. The present tank originally was located at Antonito, but was dismantled and moved here after the fire. Water for this tank is brought up from the Rio de los Pinos by a pumping station located beside the river.

Milepost No. 293.00 West of this milepost is the first (last) of the many snow fences standing today as stark, silent reminders of blowing winter snows and the old problems of keeping the track open through the long winter months.

Milepost No. 294.00 A U.S.G.S. bench mark at the milepost is 8,675 feet. Vegetation changes are noticeable as the track gradually climbs (descends) the foothills of the San Juan Mountains. Common shrubs between here and **BIG HORN** include rabbitbrush, sagebrush and mountain mahogany. Rabbitbrush or chamisa, **Chrysothamnus nauseosus,** is as common in the arid west as is sagebrush, commonly growing on disturbed, overgrazed, or neglected soils. The 2 to 4-foot, silvery-gray, bushy shrub is topped with bunches of small, golden-yellow flower heads from July through September. The heavily scented plants contain rubber, but have not been commercially exploited. A yellow dye can be produced from the flowers, and a green dye from the inner bark. Mountain mahogany, or buckbrush, **Cercocarpus montanus,** belongs to the Rose family. It is found throughout the west at elevations between 4,500 and 9,000 feet. It blooms in the early spring, bearing yellowish or dull-white flowers. This is a favorite browse plant for deer and elk. A reddish-brown dye can be made from the stout, dark-brown branches. The seeds are attached to beautiful silvery-white, spiral-shaped plumes, which contract and expand with changes in moisture, acting as corkscrews to bury the seeds in the ground.

Milepost No. 294.65 Snow fence on south side of track. The tallest trees in this area are ponderosa pines, which are the dominant trees of mesas, foothills, and south slopes of the Montane Zone (see Nature Notes, p. 63). The long needles, bright reddish-brown bark, and the large drooping cones make this tree easy to identify. Other trees that dot the hillsides include junipers, pinon pine, and a few firs and spruce.

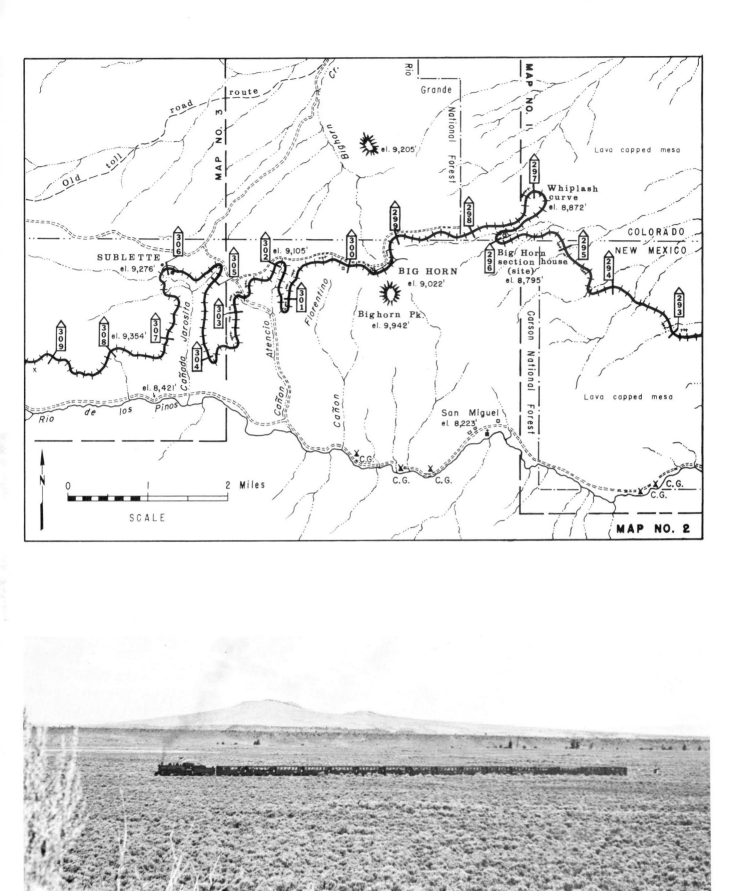

Westbound C&TS passenger train crossing a basalt-capped mesa just before reaching Lava tank. Los Mogotes Peak, el. 9,818 feet, is on the skyline. Big sagebrush, rabbitbrush, and other plants in the foreground are characteristic of vegetation in high mountain valleys of the Transition Zone.   (Ed Osterwald)

Lava phone booth. A number of these booths were located along the track so that section workers and train crews could communicate with officials, and report any trouble along the line. For no apparent reason, this booth was torn down by unknown persons (obviously not rail fans!) about 1973. (D. B. Osterwald)

View northward of the three levels of track in the "three-ply" or Whiplash, showing Big Horn section house. The picture was taken by W. H. Jackson, probably in the mid 1880's. Engine 107, a 4-4-0 type locomotive, carries an air reservoir for air brakes on the rear of the tender. The consist of the westbound train includes a baggage-express car, a coach, and one Pullman with panelled sides. On the far side of the lowest track near the left side of the picture is a rectangular stone post which probably is an early marker for the Colorado-New Mexico state boundary. The bunk house is on the left. Notice the hand-hewn ties (many in need of replacement) and the lack of track ballast. (State Historical Society of Colorado)

Milepost No. 295.08 to 295.98 The track crosses the Colorado-New Mexico state boundary three times. Excellent view of the **WHIPLASH CURVE**, and the site of **BIG HORN SECTION HOUSE**, el. 8,795 feet, is in this valley. At one time an eating house for passengers, and structures to house railroad workers were located here. Grading was completed to Big Horn on May 31, 1880, and the line was open for business this far on June 30, 1880. Whiplash Curve was called the "three-ply" in the late 1880's.

Milepost No. 296.00 Elevation at the milepost is 8,790 feet. Cross a 3-panel pile trestle 48 feet long, the lowest reverse curve on the Whiplash. Good view down the valley. Another quote by the correspondent of that first excursion described the Whiplash Curve:

> "Away we glide past romantic glades, whose velvety carpets of golden brown lie in folds of exquisite grace—clean and smooth as the ocean in a great swell. Pines are scattered picturesquely over glade and hill, casting sharp shadows upon the smooth turf. Now we have the rounded head of such a glade, in a curve that only a narrow gauge could describe; and now we are zigzaging up the side of a hill that bounds it on the right. The summit reached, we look down on the glade and could toss a stone upon two railway tracks, one above the other, and by which we have ascended, we standing upon the third."

Milepost No. 297.00 Northern end of **WHIPLASH CURVE**. Beautiful view of the wide Conejos valley and Los Mogotes to the north. More snow fences on the west side of the track. Now the track is on the top of another lava-capped mesa. The very dark, loose pieces of rock are from the basalt of the Cisneros Formation that probably flowed from the Los Mogotes volcano. (see Geology, p. 49).

Milepost No. 299.00 A U.S.G.S. bench mark at the milepost is 8,997 feet. Between Lava tank and Big Horn, wildflowers are more common than they are at lower elevations. White or cream-colored blossoms include stickweed, and yucca; paintbrushes, scarlet gilia, beard-tongue are red, and in the fall pink buckwheat is very common. Flowers with yellow blossoms include mustard, ragged sunflower, sulfur flower, and golden aster. Blue or purplish flowers are the bee plant, or skunkweed, several species of lupine, fleabane, and thistle.

Milepost No. 299.09 Cross Colorado-New Mexico state boundary.

Milepost No. 299.41 **BIG HORN WYE**, el. 9,022 feet. This station has a 1,184-foot siding and a long, curving wye, portions of which have not been used in many years. The tail of this wye was extended during the 1950's to accommodate long pipe and oil trains that commonly met at Big Horn. Bighorn Peak, south of the track, is capped with a layer of basalt.

Milepost No. 299.70 Big Horn phone booth on north side of the track.

Milepost No. 300.50 On the south side of the track is a silver-colored metal relay box called the "Big Horn Bell", or the "Big Horn Enunciator". This device, used by the Rio Grande

as late as 1964, rang a bell in the depot in Alamosa to inform the trainmaster that a train had passed this point. No. C.T.C. or radios were ever used by the Rio Grande on this branch.

This location is often a photo stop. The train has climbed a steady 1½ percent grade most of the way from Antonito. During the oil boom in the San Juan Basin, one K-36 engine could pull 36 loaded freight cars up this grade. Many snow fences were necessary along this part of the track.

Milepost No. 301.20 South end of sharp curve, one of several convolutions the track makes to gain (lose) elevation. Throughout this portion of the line, quaking aspens, **Populus tremuloides**, are the dominant trees. These graceful, slender trees with a whitish-gray bark sometimes grow to 80 feet tall. Because the bright green leaves are attached to a leaf stalk that is long and flat, the leaves tremble in the slightest breeze. These trees are widespread in the Rocky Mountains wherever there is enough water. They are called "quakies", "poples", and several other names in various localities. Beavers are very fond of aspen wood for food and lodging. The soft white wood is used in industry for pulp, excelsior, boxes, and matches.

Milepost No. 301.90 Northern end of curve at the head of Cañon Atencio. The gentle slopes and open hillsides adjacent to thick aspen groves are a decided change from the "flats" near Antonito. The groves of quaking aspens are spectacular in the fall when the leaves turn brilliant yellow or red colors. Large ponderosa pines also grow throughout this area. San Antonio Peak, on the southeastern skyline, is still visible, an outstanding landmark.

Milepost No. 303.50 Gravel pit on north side of track. The loose, rounded pebbles and cobbles were used for railroad ballast many years ago. This material is from the Los Pinos Formation, about 26 million years old.

Milepost No. 303.90 Southernmost curve on track that loops around the hill dividing Cañon Atencio from Cañada Jarosita. Nice views down the valley of the Rio de los Pinos. In September, 1880, a correspondent named Dillenback wrote a long, very flowery description of the sights along the San Juan Extension, which appeared in both the Silverton and Colorado Springs newspapers, and perhaps in other papers throughout the state. The article certainly explains why the line was built in a very graphic style.

> ". . . the Denver & Rio Grande is a romantic, ambitious and adventurous road, and must be searching for new fields and greater achievements . . . Far to the west, across the mining range of the Rocky Mountains, lies a region untouched by railroads, in whose mountains and streams are inexhaustible treasures of silver and gold—the great San Juan country. The railway heard tales of the prospectors and miners, and looked westward from Conejos toward the new land of promise. The scene could not have been more alluring. Low, smooth, gentle rising foothills, covered with grass and timbered with scattering pines and groves of poplar, extended as far as the eye could reach, their gentle slopes and flowery vales looking down upon the park, and affording romantic

views of the mountains beyond. They seemed to promise a very Eden for tourists. And the railway yielded to the seductive beauty of the foothills, and the travelers' tales of the riches of the San Juan and set out again to the west.

For miles it curved among the hills, keeping sight of the plains and catching frequent glimpses of the village. Its innumerable windings along the brows of the hills, seemed in mere wantonness, as loth to abandon so beautiful a region. Almost imperceptibly the foothills changed into mountains and the valleys deepened into canons, and winding around the point of one of the mountains it found itself overlooking the picturesque valley or canon of Los Pinos creek."

Milepost No.
304.30 Just north of a slow order (10 miles per hour) sign, on the west side of the track is one of the intriguing mysteries of this part of narrow gauge country. About 10 feet from the track is a small mound of rocks and dirt, and propped up against some other rocks is a large,

Sublette, New Mexico in the early 1900's. This westbound passenger train had stopped for water, and perhaps to let off some passengers for a summer picnic. The wooden water tank was removed some years ago and replaced with the present plug on the north side of the track. The early hand-hewn ties had been replaced by sawed ones by the time of this photograph.

(W. D. Joyce collection)

View south at M.P. 304.30 showing a cross chiseled into a slab of volcanic rock. No one familiar with the railroad has any idea who placed the rock at this point or why. Any ideas? The round black sign shows the speed limit for eastbound trains. Notice the cinder ballast in the track. (D. B. Osterwald)

flat piece of volcanic rock with a cross chiseled into the surface. Nice views westward of the track on the far side of Cañada Jarosita.

Milepost No.
305.20 Another tight curve around a small tributary valley of Cañada Jarosita.

Milepost No.
306.06 **SUBLETTE, NEW MEXICO,** el. 9,276 feet. This station was called Boydsville until December, 1880; why the name was changed is not known. The San Juan Extension was opened for travel to this point in September, 1880, but the track had been laid to M.P. 321.00. By October, a depot had been completed, and at least 100 people were living here in tents and frame shanties. One enterprising businessman had a "large" building that served as a hotel and restaurant. During the early 1900's, the section workers main contact with the "outside world" was via the railroad. Wives would ride a train into Antonito for food, supplies, some social life, and go home on a westbound train. Much lumber was harvested in this area and it is still possible to see dirt trails that lead off into the forests to old logging operations.

Originally there was a large wooden water tank on the south side of the track; today a water plug serves the same purpose. On the south side of the track is an old coal house that was moved there from Allison, Colorado in 1945. The large white frame building was a section worker's home. The hand-hewn log building was a bunk house, as was the other frame building. Phone booth No. 3 was here. The Sublette siding is 949 feet long.

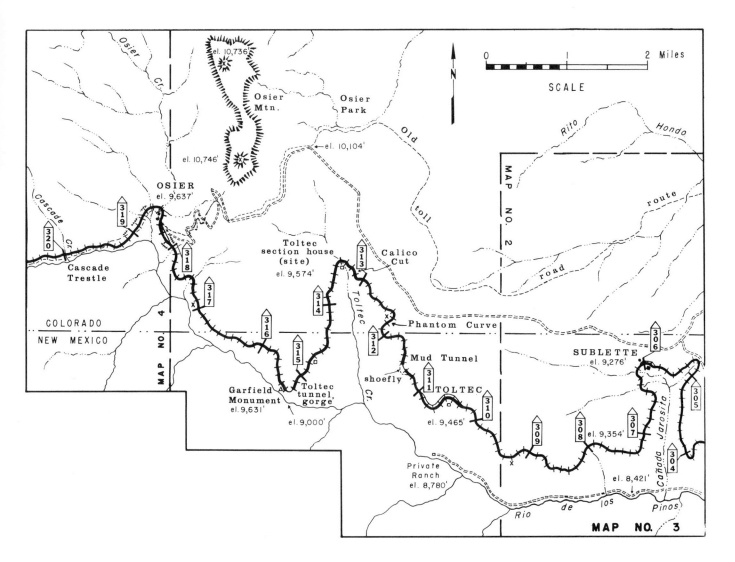

Map labels:

el. 10,736'
Osier Mtn.
Osier Park
SCALE
0 — 1 — 2 Miles
N
el. 10,746'
el. 10,104'
Osier Cr.
Old toll road route
Rito Hondo
OSIER el. 9,637'
MAP NO. 2
319
320
Cascade Cr.
Cascade Trestle
318
Toltec section house (site) el. 9,574'
Calico Cut
313
317
314
COLORADO
NEW MEXICO
MAP NO. 4
316
Toltec Cr.
Phantom Curve
312
SUBLETTE el. 9,276'
306
315
Mud Tunnel
311
shoefly
TOLTEC el. 9,465'
310
307
305
Garfield Monument el. 9,631'
Toltec tunnel, gorge el. 9,000'
309
308 el. 9,354'
Cañada Jarosita
304
Private Ranch el. 8,780'
el. 8,421'
Rio de los Pinos
MAP NO. 3

Milepost No. 307.00 A U.S.G.S. bench mark at the milepost is 9,300 feet. Between Sublette and M.P. 307.00 the track winds through dense aspen groves. Other trees include the beautiful white fir **Abies concolor.** This tall, stately tree with an ash-gray, deeply-furrowed bark, sometimes grows to be as much as 200 feet tall. The cones may be from 5 to 7 inches long. Also nestled among the aspens are occasional Douglas fir and spruce. The track is now in the Montane Zone, and during August a wide variety of wildflowers bloom in profusion. Typically, some of these are purple bull thistle, scarlet gilia, white yarrow, blue lupine and penstemon, yellow gumweed, wallflower, salsify, and orange mallow. Wild roses, gooseberries, chokecherries, and raspberries also are very common.

Milepost No. 307.30 Beautiful view eastward along Cañada Jarosita, and also southward into the valley of the Rio de los Pinos. This stream is reported to have excellent trout fishing. Between Sublette and M.P. 308.00 the track is built on the Treasure Mountain Tuff which was deposited about 29 million years ago.

Engine 483 with a westbound C&TS train near Sublette in August, 1975. The thick vegetation along the track consists of many species of wildflowers, sagebrush, and other shrubs. Thick stands of ponderosa pine and aspens are common along this part of the track.
(Becky Osterwald)

Milepost No.
308.10
A small fault near this milepost brings the Conejos Formation upward to track level. The widespread Conejos Formation, which in this area is the oldest volcanic unit in the eastern San Juan Mountains, may be as much as 35 million years old. At M.P. 308.50 a deep cut with vertical sides exposes the rusty-red, to pink breccia typical of the Conejos Formation.

Milepost No.
309.35
This long, outside curve was the site of a head-on collision between two locomotives in October, 1922. A westbound passenger train was hit by a light locomotive traveling east. The engineer of the light engine apparently mis-read his orders and thought he had more time to reach the Sublette siding. The engineer and fireman on the passenger train were killed. The remains of a locomotive pilot and coupler from one of the locomotives are down the hill about 50 feet from the nearest telephone pole. The Rio Grande apparently constructed a ramp to drag engine 169 up the slope to track level. Bricks from the fire-box and some coal are still lying along the track. Engine 169 is now on display in the Alamosa, Colo. park.

Milepost No.
310.30
East switch of **TOLTEC SIDING**, el. 9,465 feet. A phone booth is located on the south side of the track at M.P. 310.46. The siding was originally 1,166 feet long, but was lengthened to 3,400 feet during the 1950's to handle the long pipe trains that operated between Farmington, N.M. and Alamosa, Colorado. Track was completed to this point by June 30, 1880.

Milepost No.
311.00
The milepost is at the west switch of **TOLTEC SIDING**. Beautiful views of the tree-covered mountain slopes make this section of track a delight—and so diffrent from the scene near Antonito or Chama.

Milepost No.
311.30
MUD TUNNEL or **TOLTEC TUNNEL NO. 1**, 349 feet long. Watch for good photo spots at each portal, including the remains of the old "shoo-fly." At the east entrance is a large cage which was used in the popular movie, "Bite the Bullet." Much of the story was filmed along the C&TS route in 1974, using engines 483 and 487.

The Rio Grande had many problems with this tunnel, as both portals are built in soft, volcanic ash that has a tendency to slide when wet.

Milepost No.
312.10
Cross Colorado-New Mexico state boundary. From here to M.P. 316.00 is some of the most spectacular scenery on the entire trip. (Have another roll of film handy for quick camera loading!)

Milepost No.
312.20
to
312.50
PHANTOM CURVE. The track winds back and forth around tall pinnacles, spires, and pedestal rocks formed from breccias of the Conejos Formation. The weird shapes are the result of the alteration by hot water, by weathering, and by erosion of the volcanic rock. The alteration also causes the wide variety of colors seen in the rocks along this section of track.

Shoo-fly roadbed around Mud Tunnel. According to Robert W. Richardson of the Colorado Railroad Museum, sometime in the early 1900's the wooden timbering in Tunnel No. 1, (Mud Tunnel) caught fire. In order to keep traffic moving, a sharp loop of track (called a "shoo-fly") was laid around the tunnel. During the several weeks it took to repair the tunnel, eastbound and westbound trains traveled to the shoo-fly where the passengers disembarked, walked around the brow of the hill to board another train for the remainder of their journey. Freight cars were pulled around the hill by teams of horses or oxen. This view looks west along the roadbed at the eastern end of the shoo-fly. (Gordon Chappell)

This William H. Jackson photograph at Phantom Curve was probably taken in the middle 1880's. Notice the hand-hewn ties and small 4-4-0 engine at the head of the passenger train. In front of the group of tourists and the pinnacle-shaped rocks on the west side of the track is the location of the San Juan wreck in 1948. The snow avalanche came down a steep slope on the right, crossed the track and carried the coaches down the canyon. The passenger coach shown in the pictures on page 20 is at the site immediately in front of the people shown in this photograph.

(State Historical Society of Colorado)

Milepost No. 312.30 Site of a well-known wreck of the **San Juan** passenger train on February 11, 1948. The train was en route to Alamosa from Durango. Fortunately no one was seriously hurt when a snow avalanche came down the steep slope and plowed into the train at about 6:30 P.M. The lights went off as the coaches started to slide slowly down the side of the canyon and some passengers were not even moved off their seats. The locomotive and two baggage cars were not involved and stayed on the track. Most seriously injured was Mr. George Ottoway, the conductor, who was pinned in a coach by a timber. The passengers suffered most from the bitter cold. After climbing back up the hill, they were able to get warm in the baggage car. A hospital train arrived at the wreck site about 11:00 P.M. and returned to Alamosa by 4:00 A.M. the next day.

Salvage operations for the San Juan passenger train wreck of February 11, 1948. This photo looks eastward along the track toward the engine on the wreck train. The engine is backing down the track pulling a long cable through a block and tackle attached to a large rock left of the picture, to raise the coach. The cable is the faint dark horizontal line above the derrick boom. Another cable from derrick OP is also attached to the coach. The trainman in the snow with outstretched arms is giving directions to the engineer. (K. C. Flansburg collection)

(K. C. Flansburg collection)

Milepost No. 313.44 **TOLTEC SECTION HOUSE SITE,** el. 9,574 feet. Until 1942 there was a 5-panel standard pile trestle across Toltec Creek. Just west of the creek, where the track curves across the valley, is an open area where section, bunk, and coal houses stood until 1938. An 1880 water tank was retired in 1925. The remains of an old tie road are on the east side of Toltec Creek.

Milepost No. 314.00 Excellent views to the east across Toltec Creek canyon, of **CALICO CUT,** and **PHANTOM CURVE.** The flat-topped mesa on the skyline is capped by a hard, resistant volcanic welded ash-flow of the Masonic Park Tuff.

On both sides of Toltec Creek the aspens are glorious in the fall. The red and yellow leaves, and the multicolored rocks, combine to present superb photographic possibilities. Watch also for the narrow-leaved cottonwood and small birch trees.

Milepost No. 314.25 On the east side of the track are two fairly tall, irregular rock columns that resemble two giants staring at each other. The faces of these two sentinels, which appear to be chiseled out of the rock, are best seen looking north as the train passes.

View westward of derrick OP pulling the coach up the steep slope at Phantom Curve. The engine is pulling a cable through a block and tackle attached to the large rock at upper right (note cable fastened around the rock). Coaches at this time were painted green, with gold lettering. (K. C. Flansburg collection)

Milepost No. 313.20 **CALICO CUT.** A very descriptive name for the soft, rusty-red, orange, purple, maroon, or tan-colored loose clays and weathered rock, resulting from the alteration of hard and soft portions of the chaotic Conejos Formation. Avalanches and mudslides caused many problems here for the Rio Grande, particularly during the winter and early spring months when the rocks were wet.

(Ray Jones)

Milepost No. 314.32 Cross Colorado-New Mexico state boundary.

Milepost No. 314.75 Toltec phone booth is on the east side of the track.

Milepost No. 315.00 Near track level, on the west side of the train, is an abrupt change from volcanic rocks to crystalline gneisses, schists, and granites. These Precambrian rocks are about 1,700 million years old—certainly ancient when compared with the "young" San Juan volcanics which range in age from at least 4 to 35 million years.

Soon after reaching the crystalline rocks, the tracks pass beneath a "tell-tale," a tall, inverted U-shaped contraption with wires hanging down from the horizontal bar. When brakemen are on top of a car, getting hit in the face by the wires and rags hanging down, is plenty of warning to get down off the car for an approaching tunnel!

Milepost No. 315.20 **ROCK TUNNEL, or TOLTEC TUNNEL NO. 2,** el. 9,631 feet. This 366 foot curving tunnel, blasted out of the Precambrian crystalline rock, was enlarged in 1937 and is some 600 feet above the river. Construction of this section of track was estimated to have cost about $140,000 per mile.

Of the approximately 1,600 miles of main line narrow gauge track built by the Rio Grande in Colorado, New Mexico, and Utah, the San Juan Extension was one of the few lines constructed with tunnels. In 1882, four narrow gauge tunnels were built in Utah, and one in 1884 at Bridgeport in the Gunnison River canyon south of Grand Junction. Later, four more narrow gauge tunnels were built on Tennessee Pass and three in Glenwood Canyon in Colorado. With so much mountain construction, it is amazing that so few tunnels were necessary.

To return to the exciting period of construction in 1880, correspondent Dillenback again wrote a very vivid description of this portion of the line during a trip made on September 12, 1880:

"Having allured the railway into their awful fastnesses, the mountains seemed determined to baffle its further progress. But it was a strong hearted railway, and although a little giddy at a thousand feet above the stream, it cut its way through the crags and among the monuments and bore onward for miles up the valley . . . At one point the canon narrows into an awful gorge, apparently but a few yards wide and nearly a thousand feet in depth, between almost perpendicular walls of granite. Here a high point of granite has to be tunneled, and in this tunnel the rock men are at work drilling and blasting to complete the passage, which is now open to pedestrians. The frequent explosions of the blasts echo and re-echo among the mountains until they die away in the distance."

On October 4, 1880 the first excursion trip for newspaper editors came as far as Toltec Gorge, spending the night "camped" in the Pullman car. However, track had been completed westward a few more miles. The following is a description of this first night.

"Then pine logs are brought and a fire kindled, for we camp here tonight. Think of it; camping in a Pullman car in the midst of the San Juan Mountains. Our thoughtful host has anticipated everything. A royal supper from the cuisine of the Glenarm is served by waiters from the same hotel. Was ever chicken more delicious? had ever roast duck a finer flavor?

Next morning we are out betimes, some to see the sun rise and shine visibly through the gorge, others to climb and explore at will.

Breakfast is served and then we enter upon a day of unalloyed delight . . . The points of interest must be named. After much discussion the following were decided upon: The canon is to be known as "Toltec Gorge," the tunnel "Toltec Tunnel." A rocky prometory (sic) that juts out into the gorge is "Ella Cliff," in honor of Mrs. Nims."

The names chosen by this group are interesting. Why Toltec? Probably the name referred to one of the Nahuatl Indian tribes in Mexico, as the railroad had high hopes of extending its sphere of influence that far south. General Palmer and his associates had actively started construction of the Mexican National Railway in September, 1880 in Mexico City, one month before the excursion. Ella Cliff was later referred to as "Eva Cliff" by Ernest Ingersoll in his book **"Crest of the Continent."**

This early photo (probably by W. H. Jackson) may have been taken in 1884 or 1885 because the telegraph pole was moved from the edge of the wooden trestle, as shown in the photograph on the inside front cover, and because No. 100 does not have its original headlight. Engine 100, a 4-4-0, was built in 1881. The white flags on the front of the engine designate the train as an extra, possibly on a special excursion. The engine was too light for regular service. The men in the photo do not appear to be workers. (State Historical Society of Colorado)

-21-

Through the years, many trains stopped at the west portal of Toltec Tunnel No. 2 (Rock Tunnel) to let passengers view the gorge. The area was a popular spot for picnics in the early 1900's. The Jackson photo on the inside front cover and the picture on page 21 show the west side of the tunnel before the 23-foot wooden trestle was replaced with the sturdy rock retaining wall shown here. The railing along this wall was built in 1890; perhaps the retaining wall was constructed at the same time. What a thrill it must have been to ride across that wooden bridge! Notice the extra rail spiked inside the left running rail to keep any derailed equipment on the roadbed. (W. D. Joyce collection)

Milepost No. 315.32 GARFIELD MONUMENT near the western entrance of Toltec Tunnel. This memorial to President James A. Garfield was erected by the American Association of General Passenger and Ticket Agents, who were on an excursion train on September 26, 1881, the day concluding funeral services were held in Cleveland, Ohio for the President. Garfield was shot by Charles J. Guiteau, a disappointed office-seeker, in the Washington, D.C. railroad station on July 2. He died on September 19, 1881. The train stopped at the gorge, and after viewing the canyon, the members of the association held an impromptu memorial service. The association later financed the erection of the monument.

West of the monument is another tell-tale. Several hundred feet beyond that, the track is again in the volcanic Conejos Formation.

Milepost No. 316.00 The sharp, jagged cliffs that appear to rise vertically from the canyon floor are the same kinds of Precambrian crystalline rocks that are at the level of the track at Toltec Gorge. A fault trending northwest-southeast crosses the track at several places in this vicinity. The geologic map, page 52, shows the extent of the Precambrian rocks and also the fault.

Milepost No. 316.59 Cross Colorado-New Mexico state boundary.

Milepost No. 317.00 Open hillsides above the Rio de los Pinos. The slopes have very few trees because of a bad forest fire in 1879. From newspaper accounts, 1879 must have been a very dry year throughout the west. Fires also raged out of control in the Lime Creek area between Durango and Silverton, around Leadville, Colorado, and many other places.

Near M.P. 317 a bad accident occurred in April, 1881. A special passenger train with one coach and caboose left Antonito at 11:00 A.M. for Chama. The coach derailed and rolled down the hillside. Eight people were killed and six others were injured. Heavy rains caused the rails to spread on the new roadbed. There were many derailments the first several years until the roadbed had settled and enough ballast was added to stabilize the track. Another accident occurred here in 1972 when two railroad workers on a westbound speeder collided with a stationary "pop car."

At M.P. 317.11 was the first (last) of 24 wooden snowsheds built in an attempt to protect the track from snow. A total of 13,000 feet of track was covered with sheds at one time. This shed, built in 1884, was 435 feet long. It was dismantled many years ago.

Milepost No. 318.00 Cross small drainage channel just east of the milepost. At M.P. 318.10 is a large railroad cut in the Conejos Formation. Snow fences on the west side of the track indicate another area where blowing and drifting snows filled the cut, causing many blockades.

Milepost No. 318.40 OSIER, COLORADO, el. 9,637 feet. After a morning of breathing fresh, clean air and enjoying the sights, sounds, and smells of narrow gauge travel, most passengers are ready for LUNCH. Hot lunches are served from the same building that was used as an "eating house" in 1885. Picnic tables are available for all, and rest rooms are located in the former depot. In 1885 a "good meal" here cost 75 cents and the passengers had just 20 minutes to finish eating! Today the pace is more leisurely—we'll be here an hour. The fare from Osier to Denver in 1885 was $20.30.

This isolated outpost has had an interesting and checkered history. In 1878, two years before the D&RG track arrived, a small settlement was established here for the toll gate on the Park View and Ft. Garland toll road. The October 16, 1880 issue of the Silverton **La Plata Miner** stated that this toll road was the "regular wagon road to the San Juans and will be the first transportation conjunction between steam and mule power." By 1884 the area east of the track was known as "Jenkins Gardens," where Mr. William

Osier, Colorado, looking south. This photo by George E. Mellen, must have been taken before 1888 as the 50-foot Keystone turntable is not yet installed, and the trestle across Osier Creek is new and not yet filled in. The track in the foreground has many hand-hewn ties. Traces of the old toll road are visible curving west through a row of snow fences below the depot and section house. The water tank is the original one built in 1880, which later was replaced. Jenkins Gardens was located up the hill beyond the left side of the photograph.

(State Historical Society of Colorado)

Jenkins, postmaster, was also tollgate keeper as well as saloon and restaurant owner. Mr. Jenkins had a homestead and is known to have lived here until at least 1907. Crude corrals adjoined the log buildings, but no mention was made of a "hotel" for weary travelers. Location of the toll road is shown on Guide Map No. 3. From accounts of some of the first hearty adventurers who traveled over this "road"—it was anything but an Interstate Highway!

Grading was completed to Osier on July 31. The track was completed and the line open for business by October 10, 1880. According to the October 16, 1880 issue of the Silverton **La Plata Miner,** the track was still 23 miles from Chama. The bridge over Cascade Creek probably was finished and the grading to the west was being pushed ahead rapidly. Some persons estimated that about 2000 men were at work along the whole San Juan Extension. The Rio Grande had contracted with Mormon workers to help with the construction. It was hoped the track would reach Chama by November 15 to avoid the winter snows, but it was December 31, 1880 before the first work train finally arrived.

At Osier, the Rio Grande built a very small depot (now the restrooms), a large section-eating house, a bunk house, and a water tank. The siding is 1,699 feet long. A third track was removed some years ago. At one time there were also a covered turntable and a coal-loading platform; remains of the platform are

still visible today. The cattle pens and loading chute south of the depot have not been used since the early 1960's. Today cattle and sheep are taken out of the mountains by truck. A post office, established here in 1882, was closed in June, 1928.

According to the **Narrow Gauge News,** published by Robert Richardson in Alamosa during the 1950's, Osier had the dubious distinction of being one "town" in Conejos County, Colorado which was a political stronghold that managed to always muster up enough votes to control the outcome of an election in the county. "Trainmen and passengers used to sign the poll books and thus Osier could always be counted on for enough votes." Probably at no time in its history did more than 25 to 50 people reside in Osier.

The name "Osier" is interesting. No mention has been found of why it was selected as a station name. The word is a general term, formerly widely used, for willows (**Salix** species), which are shrubs or small trees.

Osier Mountain, northeastward of the station, is capped with a hard, resistant layer of lava that is part of the Cisneros Formation, the same rock type that underlies a large area near Antonito.

While at Osier, the engine is checked by the crew; then four long—and loud—blasts from the whistle summon everyone back to the train for the remainder of the day's excursion of the C&TS Railroad.

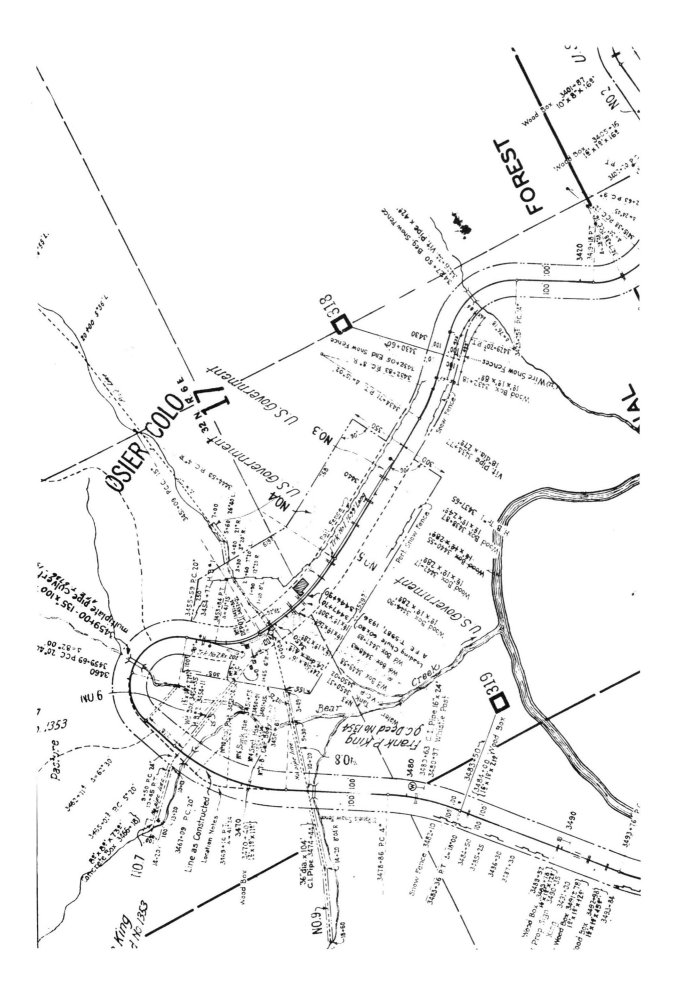

Right of way and track map of Osier, Colorado, corrected to December 31, 1936.

(Courtesy Denver and Rio Grande Western Railroad)

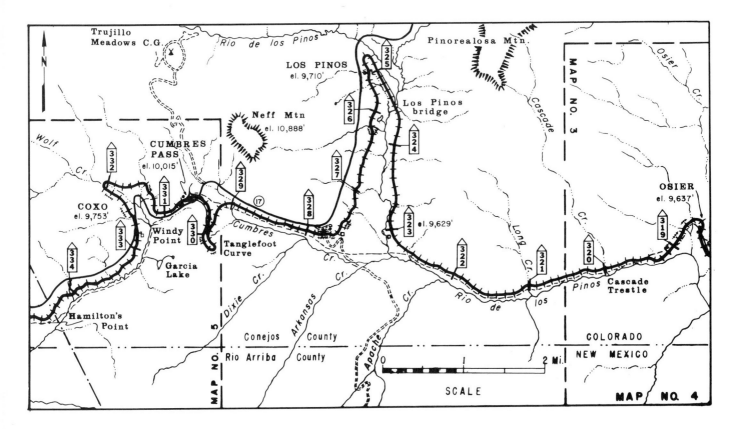

Milepost No.
318.45 Cross large drainage channel over Osier Creek, formerly called Bear Creek. Many snow fences still stand along the north side of the track. Traces of the old toll road are visible on the south side of the track from here to M.P. 322.70.

Milepost No.
319.46 Location of a 359-foot snowshed built in 1894. When it was removed is not known.

Milepost No.
319.95 **CASCADE TRESTLE.** Another scenic highlight of the trip is this bridge, 137 feet high and 409 feet long. The original bridge was wood, but it was replaced in 1889 with an iron bridge of a unique German design with bents that were tapered at each end. It also did not have any cross-bracing between the bents. In the 1920's a new 8-span, steel deck-girder bridge with steel bents placed on masonry pedestals and abutments was built to standard gauge specifications, in the event the line was ever standard gauged.

Milepost No.
320.00 Milepost at west end of the trestle. In moist areas along the track, beautiful blue wild iris blooms during the early summer. Yellow shrubby cinquefoil is also very common at this elevation, and in the late summer blue gentians can be spotted on the hillsides. Very few trees have grown on these hills since the forest fire in 1879. The track is almost level for several miles, a good place in earlier days to "make up time."

Milepost No.
321.00 Milepost on the east side of Long Creek. According to the Silverton **La Plata Miner,** the track was finished to this point on October 16, 1880. The right-of-way and track maps of the D&RGW show portable snow fences in this area. According to D&RGW records, a 374-foot snowshed, built in 1908, was just west of the

bridge. This shed was blown down by a gale-force wind in November, 1911.

Nestled among the native grasses are yellow holly grape, wallflower, puccoon, senecio, and tiny cinquefoil. Wild blue flax is common along the track in July, as is pink to red scarlet gilia, and brilliant fuchsia-colored locoweed. Purple asters are common late in the season.

Milepost No.
322.00 Nice views into the Rio del los Pinos valley. The stream is less than 100 feet below the track—quite a change from the 600 feet at Toltec Gorge! Beautiful tree-covered slopes across the valley obviously were not burned in the 1879 fire. As shown on the geologic map, p. 58, the slopes north of the track are underlain by several inactive landslides. Along the stream are very recent deposits of sand, silt, and clay, termed **alluvium.**

Milepost No.
322.95 Los Pinos phone booth on the west side of the track. (It probably was moved from M.P. 322.12 sometime after 1923.) Another phone booth can be seen due west across the valley at a higher elevation. The grass-covered valley shows the results of many events which have occurred in recent geologic time. The valley once was covered with small glaciers or permanent ice fields. After the ice melted, the area had a cool, moist climate and many landslides resulted, which give the slopes the rounded, hummocky appearance. A major fault extends northward through the valley, over La Manga Pass, into the Conejos River valley, and up the north side of the valley. Neff Mountain, el. 10,888 feet, is the flat-topped peak to the northwest. The ash-flow tuff layers visible on top of Neff Mountain are part of the Masonic Park Tuff.

Milepost No.
323.02
Site of another snowshed 287 feet long, built in 1900, which was deliberately burned by the Rio Grande in September, 1920. Another shed at M.P. 323.19 was 310 feet long and was removed many years ago.

Milepost No.
324.00
Cross cattleguard just south of the milepost. Between M.P. 324.50 and M.P. 325.20 is a STRAIGHT section of track, almost a mile long!

Milepost No.
324.52
Cross Rio de los Pinos, now a small mountain stream. The bridge is a fire-decked, 11-panel, pile trestle, 175 feet long. Just north of the bridge is **LOS PINOS SIDING,** 1,850 feet long. At the north end of the siding, the track makes a sharp, hairpin curve around the upper end of the Los Pinos valley. This long curve makes it possible for the railroad to gain (lose) altitude without changing gradient. State Highway 17 is visible to the north and west.

Milepost No.
325.50
LOS PINOS WATER TANK, el. 9,710 feet. This picturesque 1880 tank is the summer home of many cliff swallows. Look for their nests just below the overhanging roof. Until 1938 a section house and a bunk house were here. A coal house for refueling the rotary snowplow trains was nearby. This coal house burned in February, 1912 and was replaced by another one which lasted until 1929.

Milepost No.
326.10
Small unnamed lake on the east side of the track. Near this lake was another 385-foot snowshed built in 1895. At M.P. 326.19 a 450-foot snowshed was constructed in 1887. A third one, 393 feet long, was located at M.P. 326.50. Fires, either accidental or planned by the railroad, destroyed the three sheds by 1925.

Milepost No.
326.30
Site of a freight train wreck in February, 1960. Large snow fences line the west side of the track.

Milepost No.
327.00
Milepost along a sharp curve, just north of a small stream crossing. At M.P. 327.08 was an 821-foot snowshed built in 1884, the first year any snowsheds were constructed on Cumbres Pass. In 1924 this shed was replaced with a snow fence, the remains of which are still visible.

Milepost No.
327.60
Phone booth on east side of track.

Milepost No.
327.68
Another 1890 snowshed 818 feet long stood here until burned in 1921.

Milepost No.
327.80
Grade crossing (listen for the whistle!) over a dirt road that eventually crosses Cumbres Creek, and leads southward onto private land which was originally part of the Tierra Amarilla Land Grant of 1832.

Milepost No.
328.00
A U.S.G.S. bench mark at the milepost is 9,858 feet. State Highway 17 generally follows the track to M.P. 329.00.

On February 10, 1960, an eastbound freight train powered by engines 498 and 497 was derailed along a curve at M.P. 326.30. Both engines left the track and turned over; many freight cars were derailed. This photograph looking northward, shows the overturned engines and relief train from Alamosa. No one was hurt except Ben Hindelang, engineer on 498, who suffered a bruised shoulder and chills from being buried in snow that was forced inside the cab when the engine turned over. The relief train has a flanger coupled between a 490 engine (facing east) and an unidentified engine. Notice the "narrowed" standard gauge truck on the tender of 497. This photo was taken by Jim Shawcroft, D&RGW engineer on the relief train.

(Jim Shawcroft)

Milepost No.
328.80
In 1890 a 487-foot snowshed was built which stood until September 4, 1921, when it was burned by the Rio Grande.

Milepost No.
329.00
Two long rows of snow fences once stood on the north side of the track just east of the milepost.

Milepost No.
329.10
Cross Cumbres Creek on a large fill. Excellent photo possibilities of **TANGLEFOOT CURVE.**

Two of the three snowsheds on Tanglefoot Curve are shown in this photograph taken sometime between 1890 and 1920 probably by George E. Mellen. The snowshed in the middle was 314 feet long and built in 1908; it was replaced with a snow fence in 1924. The snowshed on the right side was erected in 1884 at M. P. 329.85. It was burned in 1921. Notice the hand-hewn ties still in use and the burned trees, probably as a result of the 1879 Osier forest fire. The trestles were not filled in when this picture was taken, but the track was well-ballasted.

(State Historical Society of Colorado)

Milepost No. 329.76 Southernmost sharp loop around **TANGLEFOOT CURVE**, a very appropriate name for this bit of tricky engineering!

In the early years, there were three snowsheds and two wooden trestles around the tight curve. This curve also was called the "balloon loop" by railroad crews until recent times.

On each side of Cumbres Pass, the track reaches the Subalpine Zone (see Nature Notes, p. 62). Much snow accumulates in this area, and during the spring and early summer, it is a luxuriant wildflower garden. The iris, primrose, and buttercup, grow in profusion in the moist ground. The large plant with bright yellow-green leaves, that have the appearance of a partly rolled bundle of leaves, is false hellebore or skunk cabbage **Veratrum tenuipetalum.** It thrives in marshes and wet woods. This plant is rich in starch and was a valuable food for the Indians. It is related to taro, an equally important food of the Polynesians. To be eaten, the leaves, roots, and fruit must be cooked or roasted, otherwise it produces a stinging or burning sensation in the mouth. The roasted roots were ground into a flour. In the summer, watch for the yellow arctic paintbrush, arctic thistle, yellow shrubby cinquefoil, and potentilla. In August, this area is ablaze with color when the tall purple aster, lupine, sunflower, goldenrod, and fireweed bloom.

Milepost No. 330.10 East switch, **CUMBRES SIDING.** This is the closest point of approach of the two levels of track on Tanglefoot Curve, which are about 70 feet apart horizontally, and 20 to 25 feet vertically.

Milepost No. 330.48 Location of another old snowshed that was 526 feet long.

Milepost No. 330.60 **CUMBRES, COLORADO**, el. 10,015 feet. Cumbres means "crests" or "summits" in Spanish. During construction days, the station was referred to as Alta. Grading crews reached Alta September 31, 1880 and the San Juan Extension was opened for travel from Antonito to Cumbres (or Alta) on December 15, 1880. When the D&RG completed the line over Cumbres, it was one of the highest railroad tracks in the United States.

Cumbres Pass, a narrow gap in the southeastern San Juan Mountains, was known to the Indians, and to early trappers and traders. It was the site of a running Indian battle in July 1848, between a group of Indians (Jicarilla Apaches and Muache Utes) and the 2nd. Regiment, Missouri Volunteers. Two soldiers and 36 Indians were killed. The scout for the Missourians, a noted fur trapper and mountain man known as "Old Bill" Williams, was wounded. Poetic justice perhaps—he is reported to have absconded with the money for a shipment of furs belonging to his in-laws, the Utes!

No trail was visible when 2nd. Lt. George S. Anderson of the Sixth Cavalry, first surveyed the route over the pass in 1874. His mission was to find a suitable route from Ft. Garland, Colorado, to Ft. Wingate, N.M., a military outpost built in 1868 after the Navajo Indians were moved from a temporary reservation on the Pecos River to their new reservation. In an Army

Engineers report, published in 1876, Lt. Anderson described in vivid detail his trip with 10 men in May, 1874 over Cumbres Pass. He returned to Ft. Garland in July along a well-known Indian trail south of Cumbres Pass. The map, published with the report in 1876, commonly referred to as the "Ruffner Report," shows both routes in considerable detail. Anderson recommended that a military road be built following the old Indian trail, rather than over Cumbres.

In the 1878 Annual Report of the Chief of Army Engineers, Cumbres Pass was shown on the included map as having a "toll or county road in traveling condition," between Conejos and Cumbres Pass. Dotted lines follow Wolf Creek and the Chama River southward from the top of the pass. Apparently the Army did no actual construction on either route.

In the spring of 1876, a settlement called Park View was laid out in the Chama valley, a few miles south of present day Chama, by a Chicago and Santa Fe company interested in promoting immigration to the area. As stated in the charter of the Park View and Ft. Garland Freight Road and Telegraph Co. (commonly called the Park View and Ft. Garland Toll Road), the company planned to build a toll road from Park View, up the Chama River, "to the most practical crossing of the mountains, thence by the most feasible route to Ft. Garland in the State of Colorado." Perhaps when this Certificate of Incorporation was issued by the State of Colorado on January 26, 1877, the Ruffner Report of 1876 was available, because the projected toll road generally followed Lt. Anderson's 1874 route over Cumbres on his journey to Ft. Wingate.

The earliest reference to actual travel over the Cumbres Pass route by miners and immigrants was in October and November, 1876, when the R. W. Belmear family managed to get over the pass by making drags of trees to keep the wagons from going too fast and tipping over. They settled in Animas City, Colorado, just north of Durango. Probably as more families and miners immigrated to the San Juans, they literally built the "road" as they laboriously moved their cattle, wagons, and horses across the mountain. During 1877 a trail, or very crude road was started by the toll road company to the top of the pass, but down the steep western side only an indistinct trail was available for those early pioneers.

Many hardships were encountered by early travelers crossing Cumbres Pass. The Pargin family started west from Missouri in 1876. They spent the winter in the San Luis Valley and during the time heard glowing tales of the rich land in the San Juan Basin, and the fabulous mines in the mountains. So in the spring of 1877, they started toward this "veritable Garden of Eden." In **Pioneers of the San Juan Country,** Volume 3, page 152, the following quote describes their trip:

"A trail had been blazed over the Cumbres Range, and in the spring of 1877 the Pargins, and Quick brothers and a few others started for the San Juan Basin. They loaded all the provisions they could haul in their wagons and began the climb over the range. This part of the journey proved to be very difficult. There was practically no trail and in many places it required six horses to pull one wagon up the slope. As there were three wagons in the party, it frequently took three separate trips to get over the steep places. The descent of the range was more difficult than the ascent. The men often had to let the wagons down the side of the mountains by means of ropes."

Mrs. C. W. Romney, editor of the first newspaper in Durango, described her trip to Durango in December, 1880. At that time Cumbres was still called Alta.

"Alta is the working terminus of the railroad, the tracks, however, being completed two or three miles farther on. A night in Alta, and in the morning we run (sic) down on a special to the end of the track, and betake ourselves to the carriage brought in the train with us, together with four splendid horses, eager for the journey of which they wot (sic) so little.

The railroad winds around the mountain for several miles to accomplish the same descent which the wagon road takes at one dread leap as it were. A little farther on and we reach the Beautiful Chama Valley.

We take dinner at the village of Chama, an embryo town of some prospective importance, especially in the near future as it will be the working terminus of the railroad very shortly."

No mention was made in this account of the wagon road as being a toll road.

The road between Antonito and Chama was used heavily during the construction period, and the newspapers in March, 1881 complained bitterly about the bad condition of the road. Again, no mention is made of it being a toll road.

The history of this old toll road is elusive, as many intriguing questions remain unanswered. Old maps show the route as a "toll road" as late as 1884 or 1885, several years after the completion of the railroad. The date when tolls were no longer collected, or when the road was turned over to the counties for maintenance, is unknown. Toll rates are not known, but probably were about 15¢ for a man on horseback, $1.75 for a 12-horse team and wagon. Sheep cost $\frac{1}{2}$¢ and cattle $2\frac{1}{2}$¢ to pass through the toll gate. After State Highway 17 was completed in 1923, this rugged old line of transportation to the San Juans soon fell into disuse.

In early years, a number of people lived at Cumbres year round. A post office was located here until 1937. The diagram shows the location of the railroad structures as late as 1936. Most were built between 1880 and 1882. There are about 3000 feet of sidings. Near the tail of the covered wye is the same beautiful little lake that Lt. Anderson and his men camped beside in 1874. The 269-foot covered wye is believed to be the only one still in use in the United States.

Just west of the water plug is a decided "hump" in the track. This is where the 4 percent grade starts (stops), which means that for every 100 feet the train moves forward, it descends (ascends) 4 feet vertically. East of the "hump", the grade is nearly level, becoming an easy $1\frac{1}{2}$ percent eastward.

One wonders how the construction crews for the Rio Grande must have felt when they finally reached Alta, looked down into Wolf Creek valley, and realized their difficult job was far from over. The sharp curves, very steep grade, rock cuts yet to be blasted, and bridges remaining to be built, were additional challenges to their skill and ingenuity. The back-breaking labor of placing hand-hewn ties on the pre-

View looking west at the Cumbres, Colorado depot and covered wye. The two-story depot is more than half buried by the deep winter snows. The order board (signal) on the depot was installed in 1888. This photo was taken about 1910 by C. R. Lively, the agent-operator at Cumbres, whose pictures were available as postcards. (W. D. Joyce collection)

View looking west-northwest near M.P. 330.40 east of Cumbres, Colorado. The snowshed covering the wye is in the background. This photo, taken in the early 1900's, shows the difficulties of keeping the line open in winter. Apparently the flanger behind the lead engine derailed during plowing operations. The lead engine has a large plow fastened to the pilot. These pilot plows were used when rotary plows were not available. (W. D. Joyce collection)

This interesting 1910 winter scene at Cumbres taken by C. R. Lively, shows an eastbound engine passing the section house (now the C&TS depot) and the wooden water tank. The covered turntable on the right was built in 1884 and stood at the west switch of the covered wye.
(W. D. Joyce collection)

This view of Windy Point shows two of the three snowsheds built between M.P. 331.28 and M.P. 313.43 to protect the track from winter snows. The eastbound passenger train is near the last sharp curve at Windy Point. This 1910 photo was one of a series taken by Cumbres Agent-Operator C. R. Lively.
(W. D. Joyce collection)

pared grade, and spiking the rails to the ties was done during December and January, hardly an ideal time to build a railroad at an elevation of 10,000 feet!

Milepost No. 330.75 Cross a wooden trestle over old State Highway 17. This bridge is an 84-foot, 6-panel, standard pile structure.

Milepost No. 330.78 Site of a 214-foot snowshed that stood until 1921 when it was burned by the Rio Grande. Apparently the company felt the sheds no longer were needed.

Milepost No. 331.00 **WINDY POINT.** Between M.P. 331.00 and M.P. 332.00, have your camera ready for the spectacular views of the Wolf Creek and Chama valleys to the southwest. The sharp curves, steep hillsides, and colorful rocks at **WINDY POINT** make it one of the most impressive sights on the trip. On eastbound trips, the engine (or engines) really labors up the 4 percent grade and the smoke pouring from the stack(s) often casts dramatic shadows on the hills. Three snowsheds were between M.P. 331.28 and M.P. 331.43; all were burned. Listen to the flanges on the wheels squeal as the train inches its way around the sharp curves!

Eastbound double-headed C&TS excursion train for the Rocky Mountain Railroad Club at M.P. 331.00 on September 1, 1972. The rugged pinnacles and spires of the Conejos breccia crop out on the hill above the track at Windy Point. (D. B. Osterwald)

From Windy Point, Wolf Creek valley shows the effects of glaciation which carved the sides and floor of the valley. Later, blocks of loose rock and soil (landslides) moved downward to form the rounded hills in the valley. Another striking feature of the Conejos Formation, in addition to the chaotic breccias above the track at Windy Point, is the mountain on the skyline to the west across the valley of Wolf Creek. Here the alteration of the volcanic rocks by hot solutions produced the bright red, yellow, and orange-colored rocks. Similar processes formed the features seen at Phantom Curve and Calico Cut.

Milepost No. 332.00 Milepost is east of a large fill across Wolf Creek. Where the track makes a sharp hairpin curve at the upper end of the valley, a number of aspen trees along the track have curved or bent trunks, particularly close to the ground. This feature is good evidence of landslides, as the trees attempt to continue to grow upright, while the ground slowly moves downward.

Between M.P. 332.12 and M.P. 332.78 were 5 snowsheds. More than 1000 feet of track was covered in about 6/10 of a mile distance. One 306-foot snowshed, located at M.P. 332.12, was not removed until 1938. The others were destroyed by fire between 1919 and 1922.

Ex-Oahu Railway diesel #19 with a passenger train at Cumbres on August 31, 1972. Rotary OM was set on a side track for display purposes. (D. B. Osterwald)

Westbound C&TS train crossing Wolf Creek above Coxo, Colorado, June, 1973. Notice the detailed masonry work in the culvert. (Ed Osterwald)

Milepost No. 332.20 **COXO, COLORADO,** el. 9,753 feet. At one time there was a section house, and 800 feet of passing track here. The building was retired in 1938.

Milepost No. 332.75 Grade crossing over State Highway 17. To the east-northeast, Windy Point and the roadbed on the hill make excellent photographs, especially in the late afternoon.

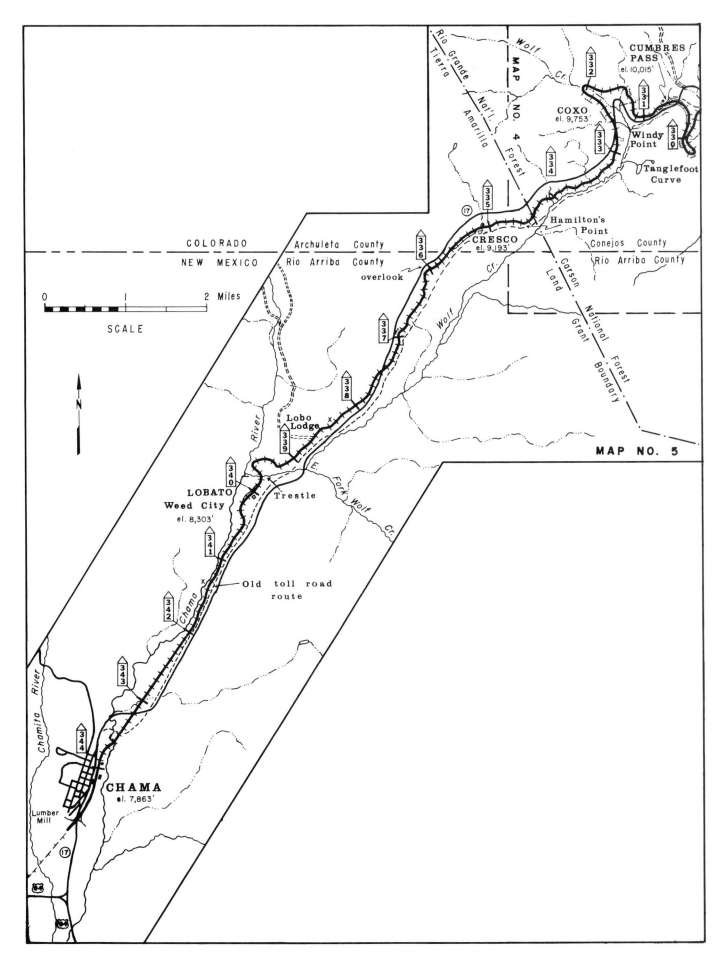

MAP NO. 4

MAP NO. 5

CUMBRES PASS
el. 10,015'

COXO
el. 9,753'

Windy Point

Tanglefoot Curve

Rio Grande
Tierra Amarilla Nat'l

Wolf Cr.

Carson National Forest

332
331
330
333
334
335

⑰

COLORADO
NEW MEXICO

Archuleta County
Rio Arriba County

Conejos County
Rio Arriba County

CRESCO
el. 9,193'

Hamilton's Point

Carson National Forest Land Grant Boundary

336

overlook

Wolf Cr.

337

338

Lobo Lodge

339

River

LOBATO
Weed City
el. 8,303'

340

Trestle

E. Fork Wolf Cr.

SCALE

0   1   2 Miles

341

Old toll road route

N

342

Chama

343

Chamita River

344

CHAMA
el. 7,863'

Lumber Mill

⑰

🌲

🌲

Milepost No. 332.85 Coxo phone booth may be seen on the east side of the track. Between here and M.P. 334.00 the train winds among thick aspen groves. These groves are a favorite habitat for scarlet gilia, blue monkshood, penstemon, and golden banner. Other trees include white pine, Douglas fir, river willow, birch, and spruce, and all add much to the scenic beauty of the valley. Occasionally deer can be spotted in the timber.

Milepost No. 334.50 HAMILTON'S POINT. The origin of this name is not known. An early W. H. Jackson photograph referred to this locality as "White Rock Point." It provides an excellent opportunity to look down into the canyon of Wolf Creek. Sedimentary rocks exposed in the canyon wall are the Tertiary Blanco Basin Formation, which overlies the older tilted Jurassic Morrison Formation (see p. 60). This means the lower (older) layers were uplifted, and then eroded before the upper (younger) rocks formed. This feature is termed an **angular unconformity**. At this point the track enters (leaves) land on the former Tierra Amarilla Land Grant. This early grant was one of many given Mexican citizens to encourage settlement on the northern frontier of the Mexican state of Nuevo Mejico.

Milepost No. 335.10 CRESCO, COLORADO, el. 9,193 feet. During construction days, a section house and bunk house were built on the south side of the track. During the 1890's, a coal house and platform were installed, probably to keep an adequate coal supply handy for the rotary snowplow trains. All of these structures were retired in 1938. The present water tank was built in 1893. The siding is 1,702 feet long. Families lived here year around, and their only continuous contact with the "outside world" was via the daily trains. In about 1909 a 45-foot turntable was used as a bridge over drainage.

The aspen trees here have been infested by millions of tent caterpillars. Many acres of trees have been either killed or badly damaged by this insect. The larvae breed in a web-like nest suspended on the branches of the aspens. Sometimes, when the insects hatch, the rails become so coated with creeping worms that the locomotives' drivers slip, and manual sanding of the rail is necessary to keep eastbound trains moving.

Milepost No. 335.60 Cross Colorado-New Mexico state boundary for last (first) time. Between Lobato Trestle and this milepost the valley is wider, with fewer trees, and more grasses and flowers growing on the slopes. There are nice views of the open, rounded hills that gently slope down to Wolf Creek. The lush grasses and wildflowers, some conifers, and many patches of Gambel's oak are quite different from the aspen groves common at higher elevations, or from the sagebrush country near Antonito. A very conspicuous, 3 to 5-foot tall spike, with lance-shaped, bright green leaves up to 1 foot long, is **Frasera speciosa**, monument plant, green gentian, or elkweed. This is a biennial plant that blooms in early summer. It has pale-greenish-white flowers, spotted with purple, that grow outward from the axils

of the upper leaves. It stands throughout the winter as a dried, brownish-colored stalk, similar to dried mullein. Most members of the gentian family have been used for medicines. The fleshy roots can be eaten raw, roasted, or boiled. Elk, deer, and cattle like to browse on the young leaves.

Many other wildflowers can be found nestled among the thick grasses. Fireweed, **Epilobium angustifolium,** is one of the most beautiful and distinctive plants found in the mountains in August. The four-petaled, pink or reddish-purple blossoms form a symmetrical unbranched stem from 1 to 5 feet tall. Fireweed grows on moist, rich soil, or on man-disturbed ground. It is one of the first plants to reappear after a forest fire, thus the name. The young leaves are excellent in salads, and dried leaves can be used for tea. The plant is valuable forage for deer, elk, bear, and cattle.

Milepost No. 336.95 Remains of snow fence on the north side of the track.

Milepost No. 337.45 Track crosses State Highway 17. The lush valley is rich grazing land for cattle and sheep.

Milepost No. 337.80 This open valley was another place where blowing snow quickly covered the track in winter. Between M.P. 336.00 and Lobato Siding, M.P. 340.00, the track is on glacial debris. The loose unsorted soil, and the rounded, hummocky appearance of the ground is typical of a **moraine.**

Throughout this valley, Gambel's oak or scrub oak, **Quercus gambelii,** grows in dense thickets of tall shrubs or small trees. In the fall, the leaves change from a shiny green color to shades of yellow, orange, and red. The acorns from this tree were an important food for Indians and early settlers because the seeds are sweet and tasty. Dried acorns can be ground into flour or meal.

The largest family of wildflowers, the composites, grow in abundance throughout this area. Some common members of this family include the sunflower, thistle, yarrow, gumweed, aster, daisy, salsify, rabbitbrush, senecio, dandelion, and sneezeweed. The most common colors for the composites are shades of yellow, white, blue, purple, or reddish-purple; red blossoms are very rare.

Milepost No. 338.35 This reverse curve, known as Hurley's Curve, by Rio Grande railroaders, was the site of a passenger train wreck on May 20, 1904. Hurley, an early-day Rio Grande engineer, was killed in another wreck on this curve.

Milepost No. 338.65 Grade crossing for U. S. Forest Service road to the upper Chama River valley. There is a fascinating rhythm in the sound of the engine as it labors up the 4 percent grade on eastbound trips. On westbound trips the engine is not "working" and the sounds are of air escaping from the retainer valves at the end of each car (See photo, p. 81).

Snow-bucking train in the early 1900's working up the 4 percent grade between M.P. 333.00 and 334.00. A wedge (pilot) plow is on the head engine, followed by a flanger and five more engines, all probably 2-8-0 types. C. R. Lively photograph.
(W. D. Joyce collection)

William H. Jackson took this photograph looking southwest toward Hamilton's Point, or White Rock Point as it was sometimes called. Whether these old log cabins with sod roofs date from the toll road days or were built for railroad construction workers is not known. The hand-hewn ties are well-ballasted with crushed rock, and the telegraph line was installed. The insulators are an early "Pony" type used by the D&RG in the 1870's and 1880's. (State Historical Society of Colorado)

This photo by Monte Ballough shows very graphically what happened to one westbound passenger train in 1904 at M.P. 338.35. Engine 170 with the baggage and mail car left the track and turned over on the north side of the track; two coaches tipped over on the opposite side of the track. No one was killed, although passengers were shaken up and had to crawl out of the coaches through a window. A relief train with a doctor came from Chama. Engine 170 was a Baldwin 4-6-0 (Ten-wheeler) and after surviving this incident, was returned to service and finally dismantled in 1926. The rails and sawed ties in this picture appear new.   (D. B. Osterwald collection)

One month before the accident near M.P. 338.35, a westbound freight piled up in the "narrows" at M.P. 341.35. According to newspaper accounts of this wreck, engineer George Lewis lost control of the train and the engine plunged down a steep embankment. The engineer suffered rib, ankle, and hip injuries, but the conductor W. K. Newcomb, and brakeman, Killian were not injured. They had uncoupled the caboose from the train so it was not wrecked. Monte Ballough photograph.

(Edna Sanborn collection)

Milepost No.
339.00
LOBO LODGE. The cabins are rented to hikers, hunters, and fishermen. Broad Spur was on the north side of the track at one time; it was used for loading timber by F. W. Broad, a Chama lumber man. The locality was later known as Dalton Station.

Milepost No.
339.75
LOBATO TRESTLE. Unlike Cascade Trestle, the original bridge was iron— early descriptions of the line mention the tall, iron bridge at Lobato. In one account in the December 8, 1880 issue of the Santa Fe **Daily New Mexican,** it was reported that the largest bridge on the San Juan Extension was completed. The report stated that it was 124 feet high, and 432 feet long. Actually it is 100 feet high and 340 feet long. The present bridge was built to standard gauge specifications in the 1920's. It is a steel, 6-span deck plate girder bridge. The walk-way and hand·rails were added in 1945. Apparently the track was completed past this bridge by December 15, 1880. The name Lobato goes back in New Mexican history to the 17th century. A man named Bartholome Lobato settled in Santa Fe in 1695 and from there, members of the family migrated to the northern part of the province. The J. J. Lobato Land Grant in Rio Arriba County probably was given to one of Mr. Lobato's descendants.

Milepost No.
339.99
LOBATO SIDING, el. 8,303 feet. First known as Wolf Creek Siding, the name was changed by General Manager Dodge of the D&RG Railway in December, 1880. The siding is 1,190 feet long. It has been many years since the cattle pens on the north side of the track were used for loading cattle and sheep onto narrow gauge stock cars for shipment to market. The depot, named **WEED CITY,** and a small fake water tank were constructed in 1970 for the filming of "Shootout."

Milepost No.
340.50
Enter (leave) the "Narrows." Glacial ice moved down the Chama River Canyon to this point. Between M.P. 336.30 and M.P. 340.00 the track is built on **morainal** debris (see geologic map, p. 60). The brown cliffs on both sides of the valley are Cretaceous sedimentary rocks.

Between M.P. 340.50 and M.P. 342.00 the track was badly damaged by new highway construction in 1969 and 1970. Volunteers spent many hours of back-breaking labor removing rock and mud from the track before the first C&TS train could move through this area. Since then, cribbing to stabilize the highway right-of-way above the track has been installed, but both the highway and track cross an active landslide, and more trouble is possible.

Milepost No.
341.35
Site of a freight train wreck on April 22, 1904.

Milepost No.
341.65
A small fault in the Dakota Formation is visible on the north side of the canyon. (see geologic map, p. 60). Between M.P. 341.90 and M.P. 343.50 is the third longest stretch of straight track—all of a mile and a half long!

This photo was taken in 1908 by Fred Jukes, an accomplished railroad photographer. This double-headed passenger train, pulled by engine 401 (a 2-8-0), was just east of the original wooden through-truss bridge over the Chama River. The tall ponderosa pine on the left side of the track is still standing in 1976.
(State Historical Society of Colorado)

In this 1973 photo, a C&TS passenger train has just crossed the steel Chama River bridge and is passing the "Fred Jukes" tree.
(Ed Osterwald)

-37-

Double-headed eastbound C&TS train on the 4 percent grade entering the "narrows," September, 1974. Rabbit Peak is in the background between the smoke plumes.
(F. W. Osterwald)

Milepost No.
342.00

Leave (enter) the "Narrows."

Milepost No.
342.50

The 4 percent grade stops (starts) here. The track is built on glacial out-wash debris from the melting Chama and Wolf Creek glaciers. Rabbit Peak, el. 8,641 feet is the rather flat-topped peak on the southwestern skyline.

Milepost No.
343.20

Grade crossing, for State Highway 17.

Milepost No.
343.60

Track crosses Chama River on a steel truss bridge 230 feet long installed in the 1920's.

Milepost No.
344.12

CHAMA, NEW MEXICO, el. 7,863 feet. The western terminus and operating headquarters of the Cumbres and Toltec Scenic Railroad. The name Chama is believed to be a Spanish approximation of the Tewa Indian name, **tzama,** which was a Zuni pueblo located along the Chama River south of the confluence of El Rito River with the Chama River. It is believed that this pueblo was still occupied when the Spanish arrived in the area. The name was used for the area around the pueblo, and then extended to the river. Another possible meaning for the word **tzama** is, "here they have wrestled." Others thought the name applied to the red color of the river waters. At any rate, when the D&RG slammed rails down onto rough-hewn ties in their effort to reach the mining camps of the San

Juans, Chama, although largely a tent town, became an important point on the San Juan Extension. Grading crews camped in Chama by the end of September, 1880.

Chama is a railroad town. It was planned to be a division point on the line. Facilities were built to service engines before going west to Durango, or east up "the hill." It is difficult to ascertain just when the first train arrived in the new "town," but according to the Annual Report of the D&RG for 1880, issued in April or May, 1881, the track reached Chama December 31, 1880 and the line was fully open for business by January 18, 1881. No mention of this fact appears in the New Mexican newspapers. The **Daily New Mexican** for March 25, 1881 reported that "stages now leave Chama at the railroad station for Pagosa Springs, Animas City, and Silverton." As railroad construction continued westward, Chama became the rail-head, and soon construction started on permanent buildings on the railroad property. The roundhouse, water tank, sandhouse, and coaling tower all are long-standing structures that help give Chama the appearance and flavor of a "railroad town."

As the train slowly pulls to a stop in front of the depot, after the last echo of the whistle and bell have faded away, and smoke no longer pours from the stack, remember the sights, sounds, and smells of your day on the narrow gauge. Think back also, of how it must have been to travel this route a century ago, and be thankful that this bit of western Americana has been preserved for future generations to enjoy.

Chama, New Mexico in 1924. At this time a spur track west of the main track was used for extra gang workers living in outfit cars. Some of the cars are still lettered D&RG, but a few have been relettered D&RGW.

Ex-coach 0506 (second car from right) was still used in work train service on the D&RGW Silverton branch in 1976.

(Edna Sanborn collection)

The 64-mile trip by train between Antonito and Chama takes 5½ to 6 hours of leisurely travel, in contrast to the 48-mile trip to Antonito by bus or automobile which takes about an hour. Obviously, one must be alert to enjoy the scenery from a speeding bus or car; therefore, a guide to the points of interest should be generalized. If one has even a general idea of why the mountains appear as they do, the trip is much more interesting. To help one understand the scenery, Guide Maps 1, 2, and 5 show portions of the highway, and are keyed to the following descriptions.

CHAMA, NEW MEXICO. Chama has been largely dependent upon the railroad for a long time. In 1886, the lumber industry began to grow in Chama and in other towns farther west. The first hand-hewn ties laid by the D&RG when the Extension was built, soon rotted because they were untreated, so lucrative contracts were available to supply the railroad with new treated ties. Lumber mills were established and the "Chama pineries" gained a widespread reputation for supplying excellent timber products. As the timber close to town was logged off, small branch logging railroads were built to bring timber to the mills. Some

of these railroads were operated by the logging companies and some by the D&RG. At least 5 lumber companies built narrow gauge spurs from the D&RG track near Chama to large stands of virgin timber. Some of these companies continued in operation until the early 1930's. One mill still operates in Chama.

Today the population of Chama is about 950 and the economy is diversified. Cattle and sheep ranching have always been important; the highway passes through cattle grazing land for much of the 48-mile trip. Large water reclamation projects in the 1960's, and a small oil field west of Chama have brought new people into town. Many visitors now come for the excellent hunting, fishing, hiking, camping, and snowmobiling available nearby in the National Forests. Chama is locally called the "snowmobiling capital of New Mexico." So the little settlement along the Chama River, started in 1880 when the D&RG Railway arrived, has survived many economic reverses, but today is proud to the the headquarters for the Cumbres and Toltec Scenic Railroad. This new railroad is a vital part of the towns' heritage, as was its predecessor, the D&RGW.

DEPOT, CUMBRES AND TOLTEC SCENIC RAILROAD. The highway leaves (enters) Chama on Terrace Avenue and crosses the Chama River north of town. The paved highway parallels the C&TS track for about 19 miles to the Los Pinos water tank in the upper Rio de los Pinos valley. The first automobile road between Chama and Antonito, generally followed the same route as the present road and was finished in 1923. Widening and re-alignments were started by the two states in the late 1960's, and the paving was completed in the early 1970's. Until this new highway was completed, Cumbres Pass was closed every winter by deep snow.

CROSS CHAMA RIVER AND C&TS TRACK. On the east side of the road is a high metal fence that extends for about 25 miles to the northeast. This fence was built by a cattle company to divert elk herd migrations. The 11-foot steel posts are set in concrete. Total cost of this project is reported to have been about $345,000.00. Rabbit Peak, el. 8,641 feet, is visible on the southwestern skyline.

"THE NARROWS." About 3 miles north of Chama, the highway and railroad enter (leave) a narrow portion of the Chama River valley. Brown ledges of the Dakota sandstone (sedimentary) are visible on each side of the road. Across the river, a small fault in the Dakota Sandstone is visible from the highway. The down-thrown block is on the north (photo, p. 61).

Many problems for the C&TS and the State Highway Department resulted from the new highway alignments that were begun in 1969; most were caused because the highway and railroad are cut into unstable glacial outwash material and landslide debris. Beneath this material are Mesozoic sedimentary layers. Several roadcuts have exposed these Mesozoic rocks (see Geologic Map No. 5, p. 60).

LOBATO SIDING. The old stockyard, the WEED CITY depot, and fake water tank are visible west of the highway, as is LOBATO TRESTLE. The surrounding hills are covered with dense thickets of Gambel's oak. This small tree is always a delight to see, especially in the fall when the leaves turn red, orange, and gold colors.

LOBO LODGE. This resort is about 5 miles north of Chama. About ½ mile north of this cluster of cabins, a dirt U. S. Forest Service road goes northward to the upper Chama River valley. The highway is built on glacial debris (moraines) from the Chama glacier.

CROSS C&TS TRACK. This crossing is about 2 miles north of Lobo Lodge. The road continues to climb toward (descend from) Cumbres Pass. One mile beyond the track-crossing is a large highway turn-out on the east side of the road. This is a great place to watch trains winding back and forth below the highway, around the sharp curves near M.P. 336. At this point, large excavations for the new highway reactivated old landslides in the Mancos Shale. Large cracks and scarps can be seen above the highway, and the lower parts of the slides eventually may affect the railroad grade.

CROSS NEW MEXICO-COLORADO STATE LINE. Near the state boundary, the highway enters (leaves) a dense grove of aspens. These trees were badly infested by tent caterpillars. Many trees died, but others managed to recover, although most of their leaves were eaten.

D&RGW engine 477 with eastbound San Juan Express below Cresco, 1933. The car behind the engine carries mail and express. This photo shows the old dirt road that had been completed about 10 years previously, quite different from today's paved highway.
(C. H. Dane, U. S. Geological Survey)

CRESCO, COLORADO. This railroad siding is below the highway, hidden in the aspen trees on the steep slope. Glimpses of the passing track and water tank are possible in a few places. In New Mexico, the highway is in Rio Arriba County. Between the state line and the NATIONAL FOREST-TIERRA AMARILLA Land Grant boundary, the highway is in Archuleta County, Colorado. Farther east, the road is in Conejos County.

As the highway continues along the slopes of Wolf Creek valley, the hills on the skyline to the east, are volcanic rocks of the Conejos Formation. The sloping, rounded hills below the cap rock are mostly landslide material dating from the melting of the last glaciers. In some places the highway is built on landslide material. The wildflowers along this portion of the highway are dazzling in August and September. Fireweed, purple aster, yellow sunflower, and goldenrod all blend together in a colorful mosaic.

CROSS C&TS TRACK. COXO SIDING was up the valley about ½ mile. The view north and northwest from this highway crossing is spectacular. The tall pinnacles, spires, and jumbled masses of the Conejos Formation ahead stand as a stark, foreboding barrier. The thin trace of the railroad grade is visible in the colorful cuts as the summit of the 4-percent grade is reached at WINDY POINT. Before the new highway was built, a dirt road crossed Wolf Creek and climbed the north-facing slope opposite Windy Point. The highway is now below the railroad track. Before the highway curves sharply across Wolf Creek, a good view of a colorful alteration zone in the Conejos Formation is visible in the distant hills to the west.

CUMBRES PASS, COLORADO. Elevation 10,015 feet. CUMBRES STATION of the C&TS railroad is west of the highway. The present highway crosses the railroad track near the location of the original D&RG depot destroyed in the 1950's. The present depot, a yellow building west of the highway, was a section house for D&RGW workers and their families. The old, weather-beaten snowshed covering the railroad wye is the only snowshed left on the San Juan Extension of the D&RG. It may be one of the few remaining covered wyes still used in the country. The "wye" is a piece of track laid like the letter Y, but with the top arms of the 'Y' linked. With this track arrangement, it is a simple matter to turn a locomotive around. Cumbres was a busy place for many years, especially during the oil boom in the San Juan Basin of New Mexico in the 1950's. Additionally, oil was carried from the Gramps oil field northwest of Chama in narrow gauge tank cars, to the refinery at Alamosa. At Cumbres, helper engines were cut out of the freight train, turned on the wye, and returned to Chama. Many westbound trains also had helpers which were switched out, and after servicing, were sent to Chama or Alamosa.

A short distance north of Cumbres Pass, a U. S. Forest Service dirt road goes northwest to TRUJILLO MEADOWS RESERVOIR AND CAMPGROUND. Trout fishing is excellent in both the reservoir and the stream.

East of the pass, the highway is built on the slope above the railroad track. There are many turn-outs here where one can park and watch C&TS trains snake around the tight curves of TANGLEFOOT CURVE, to the south. Three miles east of Cumbres Pass, the highway curves around a hill and enters (leaves) the Los Pinos valley. Glimpses of the railroad track are visible through the trees east of the highway.

On May 2, 1928 this group of residents from the San Luis Valley attempted to shovel out a large snowbank just east of the summit of Cumbres Pass so they could journey on to Chama. (W. D. Joyce collection)

Engine 484 with a westbound C&TS train at the west switch of Los Pinos siding, September 1, 1972. The flat valley is covered by stream alluvium; the rounded hills above the train are made up of landslide deposits. The mountains on the skyline are Conejos Formation volcanics.

(Ed Osterwald)

LOS PINOS WATER TANK. Between Chama and Antonito there were originally 7 water tanks along the route; 4 tanks and 2 standpipes remain for use by the C&TS railroad. Near the water tank, the highway makes a wide curve and leaves (enters) the Los Pinos valley. On the east-west portion of the highway, just before the road curves north, is an excellent view southward of the Los Pinos valley. Road cuts on the north side of the highway expose the Treasure Mountain Tuff. Neff Mountain, el. 10,888 feet, on the western skyline, is capped with Masonic Park Tuff. Rio de los Pinos meanders back and forth across the alluvium-filled valley. The gentle, rounded hills near the bottom of the west side of the valley are landslide deposits.

State Highway 17 continues northward (southward) along the north fork of the Rio de los Pinos. The long, north-south trending mountain to the east is PINOREALOSA MOUNTAIN. The highest point on the ridge is 10,965 feet above sea level. The name "Pinorealosa" means "land of many spruces" in Spanish. This area was ravaged by fire in 1879. On the slopes of the mountain, the Treasure Mountain Tuff is visible, and the Masonic Park Tuff crops out in ridges at the top of the mountain, but most cannot be seen from the highway.

On the west side of the highway, signposts point out motor trails to GROUSE CREEK and to the RED LAKE TRAIL.

The highway is built on glacial debris. The roadcuts contain well-rounded cobbles, boulders, and pebbles, comprising fine, ground-up rock material called glacial **till**, the substance in moraines.

LA MANGA PASS. Elevation 10,230 feet above sea level. La Manga is Spanish for "sleeve," a very appropriate name for this narrow divide. During the winter, the Pass is a favorite place for snowmobilers to unload their equipment for a day of touring in the deep snow.

SPRUCE HOLE U. S. FOREST SERVICE ROAD. This dirt road is about ½ mile north of the summit, on the east side of the highway. Between the top of La Manga Pass and the Conejos River, the highway descends (ascends) a steep 7 percent grade.

About half-way between the top of the Pass and the Conejos valley, the highway makes several sharp switchbacks, all of which are built on unstable landslide debris. The highway cuts contain a jumbled mass of mixed landslide and glacial debris, including both angular-shaped and rounded cobbles, boulders, and gravel contained in finer-grained material.

Watch for places along the highway where the lower portions of aspen trees curve inward toward the ground and gradually straighten upwards. This growth pattern indicates unstable ground. The highway department has devoted much time and money repairing this area, and has planted grass on the steep slopes to stabilize the surfaces of the cuts. Perhaps the old toll road route would have been a better location for the highway!

Near the sharp switchbacks, there are several turn-outs to view the beautiful, wide, U-shaped, glaciated Conejos River valley. The cliffs on each side of the valley expose volcanic rocks of the Conejos Formation, which are from 1000 feet to 4000 feet thick and extend two-thirds of the distance up the sides of the canyon walls. The younger Treasure Mountain Tuff overlies the Conejos Formation, and some Masonic Park Tuff crops out at the top of the cliffs.

The dense forest on the north-facing slopes of the Conejos valley contains thick stands of fir, and spruce, some pine, many aspen, willow, and birch. Wildflowers are abundant along the highway in August and September. The colors of the different species blend with one another to form a carpet that appears much like an oriental rug. Great color photo possibilities!

ELK CREEK CAMPGROUND and **BRIDGE OVER CONEJOS RIVER.** Near the south end of the bridge over the Conejos River a dirt road leads to the campground, maintained by the U. S. Forest Service. The Conejos River is a favorite stream for trout fishing, in fact, much of it is restricted to fly fishing only.

ROAD JUNCTION. A dirt road to the west follows the Conejos River upstream past RAINBOW TROUT LODGE, SPECTACLE LAKE CAMPGROUND, CONEJOS CAMPGROUND, to the PLATORO RESERVOIR, and eventually to the mining camps of PLATORO and SUMMITVILLE, COLORADO. Colorado State Highway 17 follows the river eastward, from this road junction, to Antonito. To the south, the tall spire of MCINTYRE PEAK, el. 10,561 feet is a well-known landmark. The summit of McIntyre Peak is composed of Masonic Park Tuff, which is underlain by steep slopes of the Treasure Mountain Tuff.

PONDEROSA MOTEL AND TRAILER PARK, MOUNTAIN SHADOWS RANCH, AND MENK-HAVEN RANCH. These camping facilities are south of the highway along the river. Along each side of the valley are outcrops of the Conejos Formation.

SHEEP CREEK. This point-of-interest signpost is on the south side of the highway. Along a wide curve opposite Sheep Creek a **terminal moraine,** once dammed the valley. The debris in the moraine marks the point where the Conejos glacier stopped its slow movement down the valley, and where the ice gradually began to melt and to retreat up the valley. After the ice melted the Conejos River cut its course through the moraine to a slightly lower level than the former valley floor.

ASPEN GLADE CAMPGROUND. The entrance is on the south side of the highway. This campground is built on an outwash terrace, the alluvial material washed from the moraine by the Conejos River.

RIVER SPRINGS RANGER STATION. The entrance is on the south side of the highway. The thick sequence of volcanics that flowed outward from the higher mountain areas are seen today as gently dipping layers of volcanic rock extending to the nearly flat floor of the San Luis Valley. Near the turn-off to the CONEJOS RANCH, is the eastern limit of the outcrop of the Conejos Formation. Many tall ponderosa pines dot the hillsides. This area is much drier than Cumbres and La Manga Passes.

CROSS RIO GRANDE NATIONAL FOREST BOUNDARY. To the south is a KOA CAMP-GROUND built on an old stream terrace above the river. Osier Mountain is on the southwestern skyline.

CONEJOS CANYON INN. East of this restaurant and service station, the highway curves southeast (northwest), and then closely follows the river. A small wooden bridge (Broyles bridge) crosses the Conejos River, and the dirt road leads southward into the National Forest. Along the north side of the road, near this bridge, is a large slump-block of Cisneros and Los Pinos Formations.

As the highway continues east (west) along low hills, gently dipping layers of the Los Pinos Formation, capped with the Cisneros basalt, crop out on the north side of the wide valley. Much water is diverted from this portion of the Conejos River into irrigation ditches that water farmland east and north of Antonito. Artesian wells also help irrigate this semi-arid valley. Juniper, pinon pine, and sagebrush are common throughout this area.

LAS MESITAS. This small farming and ranching community on both sides of the highway was first established in 1857 by Spanish families. By 1867, 24 placitas or villages surrounding Conejos, including Las Mesitas, had a reported population of nearly 6000 people. The first mission church was established here in March, 1878, at the placita then known as San Juan.

The San Ysidro Catholic church stood on the north side of the highway at Las Mesitas until November 1, 1975, when it was destroyed by fire that started in an over-heated stove. The cement structure had been built in 1933 on land donated by Don Manuel Gonzales. The church had two towers and some lovely stained-glass windows. The bell, originally from a church in Alamosa, was also destroyed in the fire. Mass was said here twice a month for its 356 members.   *(D. B. Osterwald)*

MOGOTE. This small Spanish community is 1½ miles east of Las Mesitas. On each side of the highway are some very popular cabins and trailer parks, originally for fishermen, and hunters, but now accommodating many railroad fans!

COTTONWOOD MEADOWS CABINS AND TRAILER PARK, GRUBBS COTTAGES, AND FULTON'S CABINS are located at Mogote. A mission school was established by the Presbyterian Church in Mogote about 1885, and a Presbyterian church is still located on the south side of the Conejos River.

To the south is a nice view of a well-known landmark, San Antonito Peak, a dormant volcano. Sheep and cattle ranches are very common throughout this area.

From Mogote, eastward, for about a mile, the highways follows the route of the old Park View and Ft. Garland Toll Road. The toll road continued northeast past Paisaje, another placita close to Conejos. The San Rafael church in Paisaje was started in 1891 and dedicated in 1893. In 1929, construction of the present church was started because the original structure had deteriorated. This 1929 church is still in use. Some other adobe buildings at Paisaje are visible to the north from the highway.

Eastward, the towns of Conejos and Antonito are visible, as are the perlite plants south of Antonito. To the west, Los Mogotes volcano stands out on the skyline.

CROSS U. S. HIGHWAY 285. Depot, yards, and parking area for the Cumbres and Toltec Scenic Railroad are south of Highway 17, near the NARROW GAUGE CURIO AND GIFT SHOP and NARROW GAUGE MOTEL.

ANTONITO, COLORADO. From its earliest beginnings as an outpost on the Conejos Land Grant in 1854, the land around Antonito and Conejos has had a long and interesting history. Droughts, depressions, and dips in the livestock market all affected the area through the years, but the population remained quite stable. Aside from farming and ranching, aided by extensive irrigation projects, one other industry of importance is the processing of perlite.

Perlite is a special type of silicic volcanic rock (rhyolite) similar in composition to granite, but contains an additional 2 to 5 percent water. When perlite is heated to high temperatures (1500° F), the water becomes volatile and the rock literally explodes. A nickname for the rock is "volcanic popcorn." Perlite is mined by open-pit methods near No Agua, New Mexico and is trucked to the plants located south of Antonito. There it is heated, crushed, sized, and blended for shipment all over the U. S. In 1973, 750,000 tons were shipped by rail on the D&RGW standard gauge track. Many uses for this unusual material have developed in the past 25 years. It is used as a lightweight aggregate in cement, as a substitute for sand in plaster, and in oil well drilling. It can also be used as a filtering agent in the manufacture of drugs and chemicals, and as a sterile material in which plants can be grown.

The population of the Conejos-Antonito area is about 1200. Nearly all the residents watched with interest the start of the C&TS Railroad, and helped in many ways, since the first shipment of rolling stock and engine 483 arrived in Antonito on September 1, 1970 for the new railroad. A new interest and industry was born on that day.

Antonito, Colorado in 1913 or 1914. Judging from the number of flags flying, this may have been the 4th of July. Many of these buildings are still standing.
(W. D. Joyce collection)

FOR THE GEOLOGIST

SUMMARY OF THE GEOLOGY ALONG THE C&TS ROUTE

PRECAMBRIAN HISTORY

Toltec Gorge is the only location along the 64-mile trip where rocks of the oldest period of geologic time can be seen. Crystalline metamorphic gneisses, schists, and amphibolites, that are as much as 1,700 million years old, are visible along the track, in the tunnel, and in the gorge. These ancient rocks were invaded by younger Precambrian granites and pegmatites that are about 1,450 million years old.

PALEOZOIC HISTORY

Throughout Paleozoic time, the old crystalline rocks in this mountain highland remained above sea level as part of the Uncompahgre Highland.

MESOZOIC HISTORY

The first sedimentary material deposited in the area during Mesozoic time was the Jurassic Morrison Formation (135 million years old), comprising widespread continental sandstones and variegated shales derived from an old landmass where Precambrian and Paleozoic rocks cropped out. During Morrison time, dinosaurs flourished and roamed over vast, swampy, floodplains. Erosion of the landmass was rapid, and beginning about 110 million years ago the Dakota Sandstone was deposited onto the Morrison in many places as a non-marine coastal plain sandstone. In late Cretaceous time, seas covered the Precambrian landmass. The Niobrara Formation and the Mancos Shale (95 million years old) were deposited as marine calcareous mudstones and shales in these seas. These Jurassic and Cretaceous sedimentary rocks are visible at several places in the cliffs along Wolf Creek and the Chama River east of Chama.

CENOZOIC HISTORY

At the close of the Mesozoic era, a vast mountain-building period ensued, and the Rocky Mountains were uplifted from the Cretaceous seas. With this **orogeny**—called the Laramide Revolution—faulting was very common, and many of the resulting structures along the C&TS route were formed at this time. Previously horizontal sedimentary rocks (Morrison, Dakota, Niobrara, and Mancos Formations) were upwarped, as were the Precambrian rocks of the Tusas Uplift, a north-south mountain range between the Chama Basin and the San Luis Valley. Vast amounts of debris were eroded from the uplifted mountains and redeposited as sediments along the flanks of this range. The Oligocene (?) Blanco Basin Formation, estimated to be at least 35 million years old, was formed in this manner. It rests with pronounced **angular unconformity** upon the upturned Morrison Formation in the Chama valley.

Following the deposition of the Blanco Basin, perhaps the most fascinating period of geologic events in the San Juans commenced. During the Oligocene Epoch, volcanism began throughout what is now the San Juan Mountains. This mountainous region is an erosional remnant of an extensive volcanic field which developed upon a dissected domal structure produced by Laramide tectonism. The first eruptions, scattered throughout a large area from numerous volcanos, began approximately 35 million years ago. These volcanoes erupted rocks of intermediate composition, mostly **andesites, rhyodacites,** and **quartz latites.** In the southeastern part of the San Juan Mountains, these early intermediate rocks are called the Conejos Formation. Much of the C&TS track crosses lavas and breccias of the Conejos.

About 30 million years ago, a major change in volcanic activity occurred. **Ash-flow tuffs,** more silicic in composition than the Conejos rocks, were explosively erupted, eventually covering many of the older volcanic rocks. Two important ash-flow sheets are present along the route of the C&TS, the Treasure Mountain and Masonic Park Tuffs. Both tuffs were derived from large **calderas** located 25 to 50 miles northwest of the railroad.

Numerous ash-flow sheets are recognized throughout the San Juan Mountains. However, the activity which formed these rocks ceased approximately 23 million years ago, and was succeeded by relatively quiet eruptions of **alkali basalt** and **rhyolite** volcanic rocks. These quiet eruptions ceased approximately 4 million years ago.

The beginning of basalt-rhyolite volcanism coincided approximately with development of the Rio Grande Depression, which is a large rift zone known to extend from northern Mexico into central Colorado. The local expression of the rift is the San Luis Valley, a down-dropped fault block surrounded by mountainous highlands on the east and west. The Sangre de Cristo Mountains form a prominent fault scarp, rising abruptly along the eastern boundary of the San Luis Valley. The nature and size of this vast structural feature will become apparent as the train heads westward from Antonito.

QUATERNARY HISTORY

Other features visible on the trip are the effects of glacial ice on the landscape. Glaciers were cradled in the high valleys of the San Juans during Wisconsin time. Their downward movement carved and sculptured the mountains into the forms we see today. After the ice melted, about 6,500 years ago, the landscape was further altered by numerous landslides and talus slopes, many of which are still active today.

So put on your wide-angle viewing glasses, load the camera, and enjoy all the scenic beauty, geology, history, and railroading possible on this special day!

Era	Period	Epoch	Symbol used on geologic maps	Formation Name & Age where known.	Description of Formation
CENOZOIC	QUATERNARY	Pleistocene to Holocene	Qal	Alluvium, alluvial fans, terrace gravels	Sand, silt & gravel deposited by streams.
			Ql	Landslides	Poorly-sorted, mostly angular rock debris derived from bedrock deposits and moved downslope by gravity.
		Pleistocene	Qg	Glacial deposits	Poorly-sorted material deposited by glaciers or by postglacial fluvial activity.
			Qa	Stream alluvium less than 1.5 million years old	Isolated bodies of gravel, boulders, sand, and silt.
	TERTIARY	Pliocene	Ths	Servilleta Formation 3.6 - 4.5 million years	Thin flows of porphyritic tholeiitic basalt, with small olivine phenocrysts.
			Thc	Cisneros Basalt 4.7 - 5.3 million years	Fine-grained silicic alkali-olivine basalt. Caps mesas as erosional remants of formerly extensive lava flows.
		Oligocene to Pliocene	Tlp	Los Pinos Formation 5 - 25 million years	Volcaniclastic conglomerates, sandstones, and mud-flows derived from erosion of volcanic centers in eastern San Juan Mtns.
		Oligocene	Tmp	Masonic Park Tuff 28.2 million years	Ash-flow tuff erupted from Mt. Hope caldera. Quartz latite in composition.
			Ttm	Treasure Mountain Tuff 28.8 - 29.8 million years	Composite sequence of three ash-flow sheets with locally interbedded ash-fall tuffs from Platoro caldera.
			Tc	Conejos Formation (vent facies) 31.1 - 34.7 million years	Chaotic lava flows and flow breccias of andesite, rhyodacite, and quartz latite erupted from several volcanic centers.

~~~~~~ **Unconformity** ~~~~~~

Era	Period	Epoch	Symbol	Formation Name & Age	Description
CENOZOIC / TERTIARY		Eocene	Tbb	Blanco Basin Formation More than 35 million years old	Red to brown arkrose, mudstone, sandstone, and conglomerate.
MESOZOIC	CRETACEOUS		Km	Mancos Shale	Dark-gray marine shale.
			Kn	Niobrara Formation	Evenly-bedded limestones with minor layers of light gray limy shale.
			Kd	Dakota Formation	Two or three massive sandstone layers separated by thinly-bedded gray marine shale.
	JURASSIC		Jm	Morrison Formation 135 million years	Variegated claystone and mudstone with interbedded sandstone.

~~~~~~ **Unconformity** ~~~~~~

Era	Period	Epoch	Symbol	Formation Name & Age	Description
PROTEROZOIC	PRECAMBRIAN		PЄ	Ancient crystalline igneous & metamorphic rocks 1450 - 1700 million years	Foliated gneiss, schist, and amphibolite intruded by granite and pegmatite.

Adapted from Lipman, P. W. 1975.

GLOSSARY OF GEOLOGIC TERMS

alkali basalt. Basalts which contain olivine, as well as feldspathoids and sodic pyroxenes as accessory minerals.

alkali feldspar. Refers to feldspars that contain potash and sodium but little calcium. Common varieties are microline, orthoclase, albite, and sanidine.

amphibolite. A very dark-colored foliated metamorphic rock composed mostly of the amphibole group of minerals (hornblende is common) and little or no quartz. Most have a layered or lineated structure.

andesite. A dark-colored, fine-grained extrusive igneous rock with 52 to 60 percent silica, of intermediate chemical composition between basalt and rhyolite.

angular unconformity. A break in the geologic record, indicated by missing rock units, in which one rock unit is overlain by another that is not next in the normal sequence of deposition. "Angular" implies that a time of folding took place after the first unit was deposited. The first rock unit then is more steeply tilted than the second rock unit.

ash-flow tuff. See welded tuff.

basalt. Dark- to medium-colored mafic volcanic (igneous) rock containing calcium-rich feldspar and pyroxene in a glassy or fine-grained matrix.

breccia. A coarse-grained rock composed of broken, angular fragments cemented by finer-grained material.

caldera. A large bowl-shaped depression, more or less circular in shape, that results from the collapse of the vent area of a volcano. This is caused by the rapid extrusion of large amounts of volcanic ash, dust, and lava.

clastic. Refers to fragments broken from pre-existing rocks or minerals that have been transported some distance from their point of origin, and redeposited as sedimentary rocks.

extrusive. An igneous rock that erupted onto the surface of the earth.

fault. A break or fracture in a rock or surface along which movement and displacement have occurred.

foliation. See schist.

gneiss. A foliated metamorphic rock in which layers of quartz and feldspar alternate with layers of foliated mica and hornblende. Foliation is not as pronounced as in a schist.

granite. A coarse-grained igneous rock with 20 to 60 percent quartz, 35 to 90 percent feldspar, and traces of mica, hornblende, magnetite and other minerals.

igneous. Rocks solidified from molten or partly molten material called **magma.**

intrusive rock. An igneous rock that formed by crystallization from magma, prior to reaching the surface of the earth.

magma. See igneous.

metamorphic. Rocks that were changed from one form to another in the solid state by heat, pressure, and chemical changes, resulting from deep burial or closeness to igneous intrusions.

moraine. A deposit of unsorted, unstratified, ground-up rock debris, consisting of clay, silt, sand, pebbles, cobbles, and boulders.

olivine. A gray-green, olive-green, or brown silicate mineral containing magnesium and iron. It is common in mafic or low-silica igneous rocks—gabbro, basalt, peridotite, or dunite.

orogeny. The process by which mountain ranges are formed, or the time during which major mountain systems are formed.

outwash plain. A broad, flat, or gently sloping alluvial sheet of sedimentary material deposited by streams flowing in front of, or beyond, the end moraine of a glacier.

pegmatite. A light-colored, coarse-grained, igneous rock with large, interlocking crystals of feldspar, quartz, and micas. Many pegmatites contain rare or unusual minerals of economic value.

phenocryst. A large prominent mineral in an igneous rock surrounded by a finer-grained groundmass.

plagioclase feldspar. A light-colored silicate mineral containing sodium, calcium and aluminum. One of the commonest rock-forming minerals.

pumice. A light-weight, light-colored, glassy, volcanic igneous rock having the composition of rhyolite, containing a large percentage of bubbles formed by escaping gases. Most pumice will float on water.

quartz latite. An extrusive igneous rock of intermediate composition. It contains quartz, plagioclase, biotite, and/or hornblende as phenocryst minerals, with alkali feldspar and quartz in the glassy groundmass.

rhyodacite. Extrusive volcanic (igneous) rocks of intermediate composition between basalt and rhyolite, containing large crystals (phenocrysts) of quartz, plagioclase feldspar, and either biotite or hornblende in a fine-grained or glassy matrix composed of **alkali feldspar** and quartz.

rhyolite. Light-colored extrusive volcanic (igneous) rocks containing large crystals' (phenocrysts) of quartz and alkali feldspar in a glassy to very fine-grained matrix. Most rhyolites show flow textures.

schist. A metamorphic rock that readily splits into thin, parallel layers or slabs because of its elongated and parallel minerals. The resulting structure is called **foliation.**

sedimentary. Rocks formed by the deposition, consolidation, and cementation of loose sediment, accumulated in layers from the disintegration and decomposition of pre-existing rocks.

shield volcano. A volcano with a broad, low cone containing a central vent, usually located near the top. The lava that flows out of the vent is usually basaltic and therefore very fluid, allowing it to flow for long distances before congealing.

terminal or **end moraine.** A curving or crescent-shaped ridge of rock debris deposited across a valley by a glacier, that marks the farthest advance of the ice.

tholeiitic basalt. Basalt which generally has no olivine crystals.

till. An unsorted mixture of sand, clay, gravel, cobbles, and boulders mixed with finely ground-up rock debris deposited beside, in front of, and underneath a glacier. It is derived from debris carried in the ice.

tuff. A pyroclastic volcanic rock formed by the lithification of ash (ie., fragments less than 4 mm. in diameter). Tuff may also contain larger rock fragments blown from a volcano.

tuff breccia. A volcanic rock in which large rock fragments are set in a fine-grained tuffaceous matrix.

volcanic breccia. A lithified rock with angular volcanic rock fragments larger than 64 mm. set in a matrix of fine-grained volcanic material. The fragments have sharp edges and unworn corners.

welded tuff. A pyroclastic volcanic rock formed by compaction of hot, glassy and lithic material following an explosive "glowing avalanche" eruption.

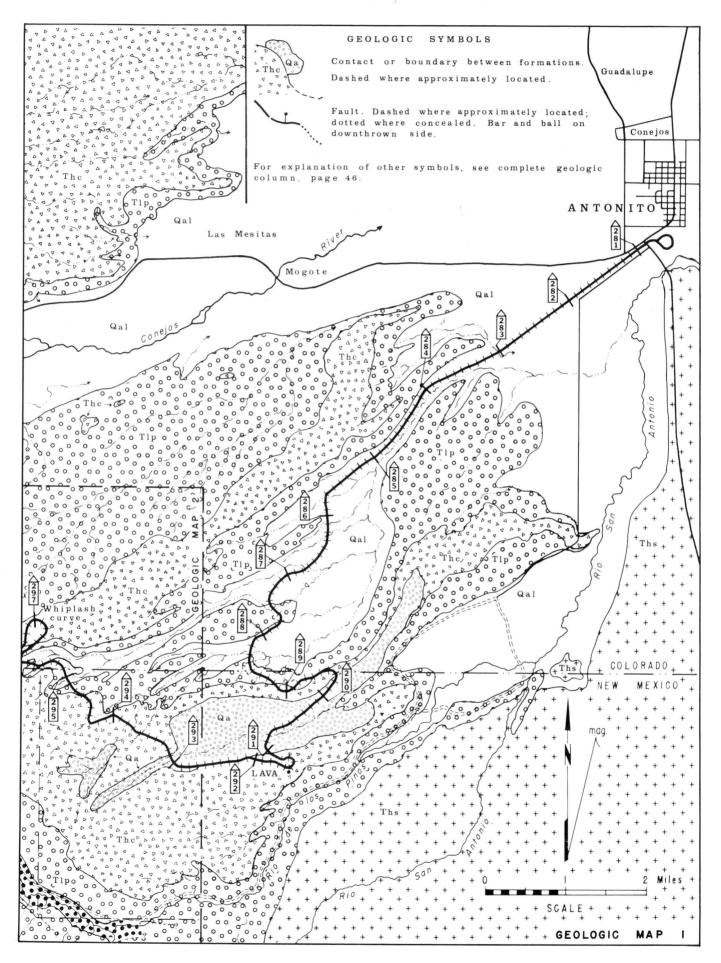

GEOLOGIC SYMBOLS

Contact or boundary between formations.
Dashed where approximately located.

Fault. Dashed where approximately located;
dotted where concealed. Bar and ball on
downthrown side.

For explanation of other symbols, see complete geologic
column, page 46.

Guadalupe

Conejos

ANTONITO

281

282

283

284

285

286

287

288

289

290

291

292

293

294

295

297

Whiplash
curve

LAVA

Las Mesitas

Mogote

Conejos

River

Rio San Antonio

Rio de los Pinos

Rio San Antonio

COLORADO
NEW MEXICO

mag.

N

Qa

Thc

Qal

Tlp

Thc

Tlp

Thc

Tlp

Qal

Qal

Tlp

Thc

Qal

Tlp

Thc

Qa

Qa

Thc

Tlpo

Ths

Ths

Ths

GEOLOGIC MAP 2

0   1   2 Miles

SCALE

GEOLOGIC MAP I

The Cumbres and Toltec Scenic Railroad traverses the southeastern flank of the San Juan Mountains, and in so doing, passes many fascinating geologic features. For this reason, a separate guide to the geology along the narrow gauge is included, hopefully providing passengers with a better understanding of the events which shaped the San Juan Mountains and produced the magnificent scenery visible from the train. The text is keyed to 5 accompanying geologic maps and all descriptions and locations are, in turn, keyed to the mileposts along the track. Technical terms are used as little as possible but are underlined where first used and defined in the glossary on page 47. Railroad cuts, as with highway cuts, are excellent places to see geologic features, so many of these locations are referred to in the text. The described geologic formations are mappable units of rocks that can be traced from one locality to another. A complete geologic column is on page 46.

Milepost No. 280.70 ANTONITO, COLORADO, el. 7,888 feet, the eastern terminus of the Cumbres and Toltec Scenic Railroad. From Antonito to M.P. 286.00 the track is built on deposits of **alluvium,** the loose, unconsolidated debris that results from active erosion in the mountains, with gradual transportation and deposition along the stream valleys, and out onto the flat floor of the San Luis Valley. At many places along the eastern edge of the San Juan Mountains, large masses of clay, silt, sand, and gravel were deposited as spreading, gently-sloping, fan-shaped masses called **alluvial fans.** The Conejos River deposited a large alluvial fan along the western edge of the San Luis Valley, just west of Antonito during **Quaternary** time. The Quaternary Period of geologic time followed the Tertiary Period about 2 or 3 million years ago, and continues to the present. (See Geologic column, page 46).

Milepost No. 286.00 At track level is an obscure boundary, or contact, between the alluvium (Qal) and the Los Pinos Formation (Tlp), that was deposited during Miocene time. Small railroad cuts in tuffaceous sandstone just south of the milepost are in the Los Pinos Formation. Other outcrops along the bottom of the valley are visible between M.P. 287.45 and 287.70, and again at M.P. 288.30. The Los Pinos Formation is composed of sandstones, gravels, conglomerates, and other **clastic** materials which resulted from weathering and erosion of nearby volcanic highlands, followed by redeposition of the debris at lower elevations. This Formation was first studied and described along Rio de los Pinos, south of Lava water tank, M.P. 292.00, hence the name. The clastic material spread outward as an apron around major volcanic centers. Some **basalt** flows and **tuffs** also are interlayered within the Formation.

In this vicinity, the Los Pinos Formation is about 600 feet thick and is about 25 millions years in age. It is the most continuous and widespread of the Tertiary **volcaniclastic** formations in the eastern San Juan Mountains, extending for many miles along the mountain front.

Milepost No. 287.00 As the train winds through this tributary valley of Rio San Antonio, the mesas visible to either side of the track dip gently eastward and are capped by hard alkali basalt, called the Cisneros Basalt (Thc), about 4.7 to 5.3 million years old. The track gradually climbs onto a mesa (descends from a mesa) where the Cisneros will be at track level.

Milepost No. 288.55 Cross Colorado-New Mexico state boundary for the first (last) time.

Milepost No. 289.00 At track level are outcrops of basalt that probably are the Jarita Member of the Los Pinos Formation, although it is not shown on Geologic Map No. 1 because it is not continuous. Along the top of the mesa, the capping Cisneros Basalt can be observed easily in the railroad cuts. The rock is fine-grained, dark brown to gray, and often contains large crystals of green **olivine,** and whitish **plagioclase feldspar.** Many cavities in the rock resulted from the escape of steam and gas during cooling. The peak visible across the Conejos valley to the north is Los Mogotes, el. 9,818 feet, a volcano from which the Cisneros lavas poured out onto the surface, in places covering the Los Pinos Formation. The Cisneros represents the last (or youngest) known eruptions in the San Juan volcanic field.

Milepost No. 290.00 From about 289.70 to 292.00, the track is on locally derived, well-rounded gravel, cobbles, boulders, and some fine-grained loose material deposited on the Cisneros lava cap. To the southeast is San Antonio Peak, el. 10,908 feet, a large dome-shaped **shield volcano.** The volcanic rocks within the Rio Grande rift zone, including those of San Antonio Peak, are younger than the Cisneros Basalt, and also differ chemically.

Milepost No. 291.55 LAVA TANK, el. 8,500 feet. A long railroad cut in the Cisneros Basalt is west of the water tank. To the southeast, across the Rio de los Pinos valley, the layered volcanics exposed in the north-facing cliffs are the Servilleta Formation, deposited between 3.6 to 4.5 million years ago, and probably are younger than the rocks on San Antonio Peak. The Formation is composed of beds of sand and gravel intertongued with **olivine tholeiite** basalt flows that accumulated in the subsiding Rio Grande Depression. These lavas were generated in a different manner from those in the San Juan Mountains.

Between Lava Tank and M.P. 296.00, the track winds across a fairly flat mesa capped by the Cisneros Basalt, crosses the Los Pinos Formation several times, and locally crosses some alluvium (Qa) that is younger than that near Antonito.

Milepost No. 295.08 Cross Colorado-New Mexico state boundary—and then cross it two more times before reaching M.P. 296.00.

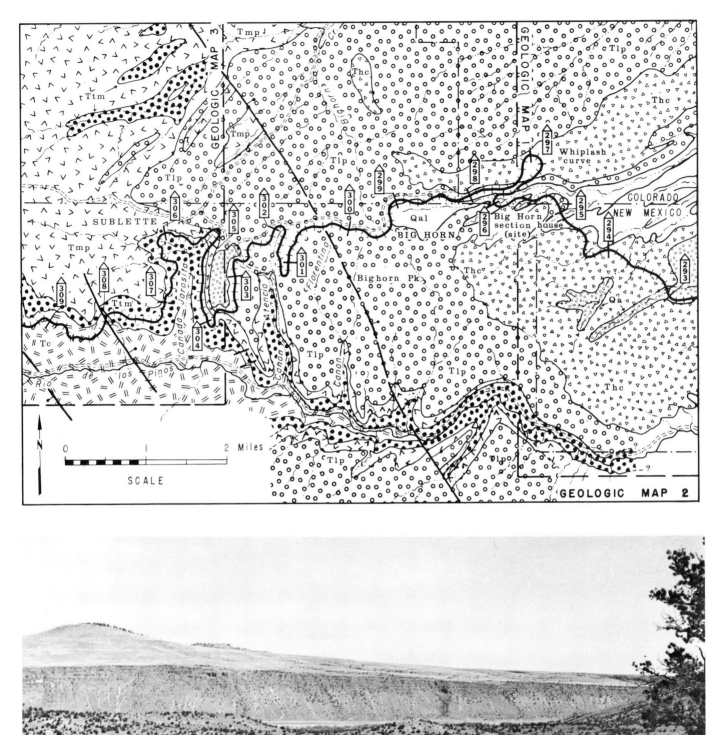

View north from M.P. 297.00 showing Los Mogotes volcano on the skyline, the Conejos River valley in the middle distance, and the layered eastward-dipping volcanic rocks exposed in the cliffs rimming the mesa below Los Mogotes. State Highway 17 is in the Conejos River valley.

(D. B. Osterwald)

Milepost No.
296.00
BIG HORN SECTION HOUSE SITE. Track crosses the alluvium-filled valley and climbs (descends) the south side of a mesa, beside outcrops of the Los Pinos Formation, and near the top, the basalts of the Cisneros. Three levels of track are easy to see from here.

Milepost No.
297.00
North end of the **WHIPLASH CURVE.** Good view to the north of the Conejos River valley and Los Mogotes volcano, about 6 miles away.

Milepost No.
298.00
To the southeast is a nice view of Bighorn Peak, el. 9,942 feet, which is capped by a resistant layer of the Jarita Basalt Member of the Los Pinos Formation.

Milepost No.
299.09
Cross Colorado-New Mexico state boundary.

Milepost No.
299.41
BIG HORN WYE and passing track. From here to M.P. 303.70, railroad cuts expose soft, light-gray, cross-bedded tuffaceous sandstones and conglomerates of the Los Pinos Formation. Many gravels, cobbles, and boulders are visible in these cuts. These fragments were smoothed and well-rounded during transport by streams. At M.P. 303.50, a large deposit of this material was excavated for use as railroad track ballast. At M.P. 300.30, a large northwest-trending fault crosses the track, but displacement of beds in the Los Pinos Formation is hard to see.

Railroad cut at M.P. 303.90 showing the contact between the Masonic Park Tuff (Tmp) at the top, and the Treasure Mountain Tuff (Ttm) below. (D. B. Osterwald)

Milepost No.
303.70
Between M.P. 303.70 and M.P. 305.50 another type of Tertiary volcanic rock, called Masonic Park Tuff (Tmp), crops out along the track. A deep railroad cut at M.P. 303.90 exposes this **welded ash-flow tuff** composed of fine-grained material that was blown out of a volcano and consolidated by heat about 28 million years ago (see photo, page 51). The material in the Masonic Park Tuff probably came from the Mt. Hope **caldera** located a few miles northwest of the Summitville, Colorado mining district. Typical outcrops of the Masonic Park, along the east side of the track from M.P. 303.70 to M.P. 305.50, are the only places on the railroad where the Formation is at track level. The purplish-gray or pinkish-gray, fine-grained tuff weathers into platy or slabby pieces of rock that are visible on the hillsides above Sublette where the Formation is from 50 to 100 feet thick.

Milepost No.
306.06
SUBLETTE, NEW MEXICO, el. 9,276 feet. Along the track at the Sublette depot is the contact between the Masonic Park Tuff (Tmp) and the Treasure Mountain Tuff (Ttm), another widespread volcanic Formation. The Treasure Mountain Tuff is mostly a non-welded ash-fall tuff with some dark-colored welded tuffs, and interlayered water-carried beds of buff to gray tuffaceous standstones and conglomerates. Large boulders fill old stream channels in some places. The Treasure Mountain Tuff is as much as 250 feet thick along the north side of the Rio de los Pinos. The ash-flow and ash-fall tuffs were erupted from the Platoro caldera located about 25 miles northwest of Sublette. The Treasure Mountain and Masonic Park Tuffs were deposited during a violent type of volcanic activity that started in the San Juans about 30 million years ago and lasted until about 23 million years ago. Along the C&TS route, the Treasure Mountain was deposited on a very irregular upper surface of the older Conejos Formation.

South of Sublette, dense vegetation makes it almost impossible to see outcrops of the Treasure Mountain Tuff along the track, but between M.P. 307.00 and M.P. 308.10 are several railroad cuts in this unit.

Milepost No.
307.00
Excellent views into Cañada Jarosita, where yet an older volcanic unit, the Conejos Formation (Tc), is visible below the track. The Conejos will be at track level from M.P. 308.10 to Coxo, Colorado, M.P. 332.20.

Milepost No.
308.10
Cross a small northwest-trending fault that brings the Conejos Formation upward to track level. This Formation was first described along the Conejos River, 3 miles downstream from Platoro, Colorado. The spectacular spires, pinnacles, pedestals, and jumbled masses of brightly colored rocks visible from here to Coxo, M.P. 332.20, are entirely within the Conejos Formation—a very photogenic area and rock type.

The Conejos Formation, one of the oldest volcanic sequences in the San Juan volcanic field, began forming from numerous volcanoes as early as 34 million years ago and stopped erupting about 30 million years ago. During that time, great quantities of intermediate

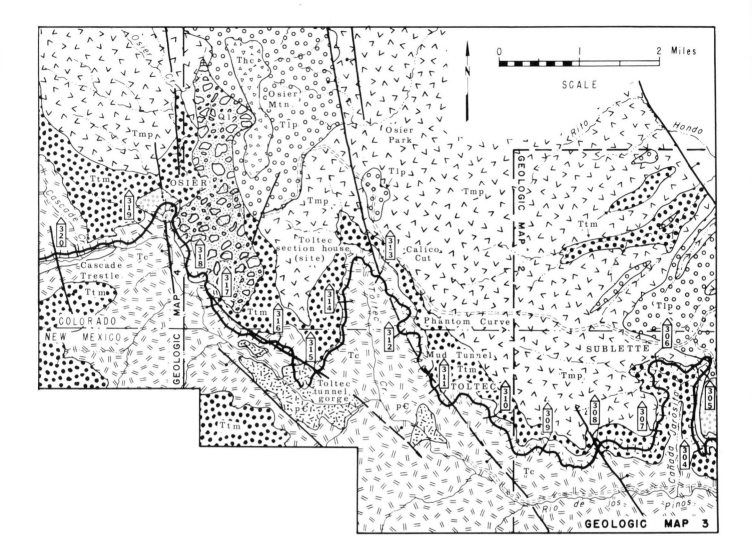

GEOLOGIC MAP 3

composition lava flows, flow **breccias,** and explosive **tuff breccias** were erupted. Those rocks are interlayered with conglomerates and tuffaceous sandstones derived from erosion of volcanic centers in southern Colorado. These eruptions were more passive than the explosive types that formed the younger Treasure Mountain and Masonic Park Tuffs. Rock types in the Conejos include **alkili andesite, rhyodacite,** and **mafic quartz latite.** The Conejos rocks were deposited upon an rough eroded upland surface. The Formation varies in thickness along the route of the C&TS railroad, ranging from 1000 feet west and northwest of Toltec Gorge, to about 4000 feet thick elsewhere in the eastern San Juans.

Between M.P. 308.10 and M.P. 309.00 the train passes tall, massive cliffs and spires resulting from erosion of the Conejos breccias. Large, angular fragments of igneous rock are easy to see in the rusty red to pink cliffs.

Milepost No. 310.30 East switch of **TOLTEC SIDING.** The rocks visible at track level locally appear to have been burned, and changed by heat from younger (overlying) lava flows. There is also much alteration of the Conejos rocks along a fault that trends northwest on the east side of the valley of Toltec Creek.

Milepost No. 311.00 West switch of **TOLTEC SIDING.** Toltec Creek valley follows a large fault (See Geologic Map No. 3) that parallels the railroad track for several miles. Because of this fault, the Conejos Formation breccias were chemically changed by weathering, alteration, circulating ground waters and other processes, and are now a soft mud that flows easily when wet. These mudflows caused many problems for the D&RGW in past years. During periods of heavy rain, this unstable material slips and flows onto the track.

Milepost No. 311.30 **MUD TUNNEL,** 349 feet long.

Milepost No. 312.10 Cross Colorado-New Mexico state boundary.

Milepost No. 312.20 to 312.50 **PHANTOM CURVE.** This is one of the most spectacular sections of track along the C&TS route. It has been photographed from nearly every conceivable angle since W. H. Jackson took the photographs shown on page 54 and 55 in the 1880's. The chaotic breccias and conglomerates that form the weird shapes, pedestal rocks, and jumbled outcrops are the result of alteration by hot waters and by weathering of the hard and soft breccias. The wide variety of colors is due to chemical changes in the rocks. A deep cut near M.P. 312.00 is a good place to see these Conejos breccias.

Milepost No. 313.20 **CALICO CUT.** This cut shows the results of faulting and hydrothermal alteration of the Conejos breccias. The colors range from red to orange to purple to tan. Many mud slides have occurred along this section of track.

Milepost No. 313.44 **TOLTEC SECTION HOUSE SITE,** el. 9,574 feet. Cross Toltec Creek.

Milepost No. 314.00 The contact or boundary between the Conejos Formation and the Treasure Mountain Tuff is on the cliff above the track between M.P. 314.00 and the telephone box east of Tunnel No. 2 (Rock Tunnel). Some loose rocks from the Treasure Mountain Tuff also are scattered on the hillsides and along the track; this is a good opportunity to compare the two types of rock. To the east and northeast, the Conejos outcrops of Phantom Curve and Calico Cut form dramatic gashes on the slopes of Toltec Creek canyon. High above the track on the skyline, outcrops of Masonic Park Tuff cap the mesa. Below the Masonic Park is the Treasure Mountain Tuff, which in turn rests upon the Conejos Formation.

Milepost No. 314.25 On the east side of the track are two erosional remnants (pedestal rocks) of the Conejos Formation that resemble two people looking intently at each other. In the valley below are thick ledges of the Conejos.

Milepost No. 314.32 Cross Colorado-New Mexico state boundary.

Milepost No. 315.20 **ROCK TUNNEL** or **TOLTEC TUNNEL NO. 2** and **TOLTEC GORGE.** At M.P. 315.00 the track crosses a fault contact between ancient Precambrian crystalline rocks (P€) and the Tertiary Conejos Formation (Tc). Many outcrops of these crystalline **metamorphic** and **igneous** rocks are visible along the track, inside the tunnel, and in Toltec Gorge. The metamorphic rocks are about 1,700 million years old, and were intruded by igneous rocks that are a mere 1,450 million years old.

These crystalline igneous and metamorphic rocks were exposed by erosion following mountain uplift at the end of the Cretaceous Period, about 70 million years ago. At that time, this entire region was a broad northwest-trending highland about 300 miles long. Large-scale faulting accompanied the uplift and continued into the Tertiary Period, bringing the crystalline rocks into contact with much younger volcanic rocks. Some of these faults are shown on the geologic maps.

The rocks along the track and downward into Toltec Gorge are metamorphic **gneiss, schist,** and **amphibolite** that were intruded by younger **granite** and **pegmatite.**

Milepost No. 315.60 Fault contact of the Precambrian with the Conejos Formation at track level. From Toltec Tunnel No. 2, to M.P. 316.40 are

nice views of jagged Precambrian rocks in the Rio de los Pinos canyon. Toltec Gorge is a very narrow, deep, V-shaped canyon because the stream had a difficult time eroding the harder, more resistant crystalline rocks.

Milepost No. 317.00 West of this milepost are several deep railroad cuts in breccias and flows of the Conejos Formation and near M.P. 318.00 is a small outcrop of Treasure Mountain Tuff.

Milepost No. 318.40 **OSIER, COLORADO,** el. 9,367 feet. Lunch Stop. This station on the grass-covered hillside is built on a large landslide (Ql) that came from the west side of Osier Mountain and along Osier Creek (See photo, page 58). The top of Osier Mountain is capped with the Cisneros Basalt; below is the Los Pinos Formation, but most of it is disturbed by landsliding. Westward from Osier to Cumbres Pass, the Conejos Formation contains successively less breccia.

An earthquake was felt by residents of Osier and Cumbres in late March, 1884. Apparently the snow was shifted about, but no damage was noted. In May, 1966, another quake occurred at Dulce, New Mexico, west of Chama. Earthquakes that can actually be felt, however, are uncommon in this area.

Milepost No. 319.95 **CASCADE TRESTLE.** Conejos breccias crop out in the railroad cuts along this section of track. Across the Rio de los Pinos are steep slopes partly covered with large, angular-shaped rock fragments which were broken from ledges high on the hillside, and which gradually slid down into the valley to form large piles of loose, broken rock at the base of the hills. This loose material is called **talus.**

Engine 483 at Cascade Creek Trestle eastbound with the first "Moonlight Excursion" on the C&TS Railroad, August 25, 1972. The large car behind the engine is the steel "Hinman" coach from Mexico. Note the tapered bents in the trestle. (Ed Osterwald)

This beautiful panorama looks southwest from the high cliffs at Phantom Curve, M.P. 312.50, toward Toltec Gorge in the distance. The track that curves out of sight to the left, is near M.P. 312.00. The jumbled, chaotic Conejos rocks on the right cliff are typical of this section of the line. The track is ballasted and the telegraph is installed, so the picture probably was taken in the mid 1880's. W. H. Jackson photo.

(State Historical Society of Colorado)

W. H. Jackson obviously enjoyed his work and always tried to obtain an unusual and spectacular view. This photograph looks west-northwest above the track from the same place the previous photo was taken. The pinnacle of Conejos Formation shows the chaotic volcanic breccia very clearly. The outfit car in the lower left is standing on a temporary spur. The men are carrying some necessary tools for early life in the west—one has an axe and the other a large-caliber rifle. They may have been working on the telegraph line—the reclining man is wearing what seems to be a lineman's pole-climbing belt.

(State Historical Society of Colorado)

View east from the ridge above Toltec Tunnel. The scar of the new roadbed on the hills to the east is hardly visible today because of thick stands of youthful aspen trees. In the foreground, the outlines of the Precambrian crystalline rocks are easy to see. This area obviously was burned, probably during the 1879 Osier fire. Today dense aspens line the eastern approach to Toltec Tunnel. Judging from the hand-hewn ties on the roadbed and the stack of ties along the track, this photograph must have been taken in the 1880's. Cross-arms have been installed in the telegraph poles to carry two wires instead of the original single wire. W. H. Jackson photo.

(State Historical Society of Colorado)

Jackson turned his camera west while standing above Toltec Tunnel and recorded this view of Toltec Gorge, the narrow Rio de los Pinos, and outcrops of badly cracked and fractured Precambrian granites, gneisses, and schists in the foreground and middle background. The dead trees standing on the hills north of the track probably were burned in the Osier fire of 1879. (State Historical Society of Colorado)

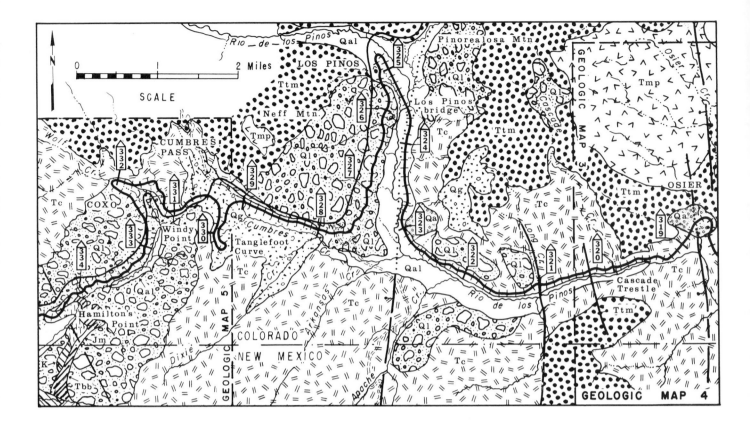

View northeast of Osier Mountain on the left skyline, capped with Cisneros basalt. The rounded slopes below Osier Mountain are land-slide deposits. C&TS engine 483 is at M.P. 317.20 along cuts in the Conejos Formation. The track crosses the small tributary stream at M.P. 317.40. This was the first excursion train on the C&TS, October 4, 1970, and was operated for press and officials of the states of Colorado and New Mexico. The old road in the foreground formerly led southward into the Tierra Amarilla Land Grant.

(D. B. Osterwald)

Milepost No. 321.00 At track level are some outcrops of light-buff to tan-colored pumice, or ash-fall tuff within the Conejos Formation. This section of track is almost level—quite a novelty! In the bottom of the valley are several nearly flat terraces along the stream. Rio de los Pinos has cut a new channel through this alluvium, part of which came from glacial debris and landslide deposits. West of the milepost are good outcrops along the track of reddish-colored Conejos breccias. It is easy to see large, irregular, angular blocks and pieces of the volcanic igneous rock cemented in fine-grained material.

Milepost No. 322.95 Los Pinos phone booth. Outcrop of the Conejos Formation beside the track. The valley is floored from here to M.P. 325.30 with alluvium deposits. To the west, across the valley where the track is higher on the hillside, is a large landslide. The rounded, hummocky, irregular slopes are characteristic expressions of the downward and outward motion of landslides. To the west the skyline is Neff Mountain, el. 10,888 feet. The cap rock is Masonic Park Tuff; the slopes below are Treasure Mountain Tuff, most of which is covered by extensive landslides.

Milepost No. 324.52 Cross Rio de los Pinos. From the north end of the bridge to M.P. 325.20 is a straight section of track built on alluvium. The Cumbres Pass fault trends north-northeast through this valley, north to La Manga Pass, across the Conejos River, and farther northward where it intersects another large fault that is part of the Platoro caldera. Most of the obvious traces of the fault in this valley are covered by alluvium and glacial debris, so it is shown on the geologic map, page 58, as a dotted line.

Milepost No. 325.50 **LOS PINOS WATER TANK**, el. 9,710 feet.

Milepost No. 326.10 The small lake on the east side of the track was caused by water that collected in a landslide depression.

Milepost No. 327.00 Track is built on landslide debris. Between M.P. 327.00 and M.P. 329.00 are several large blocks of the Conejos that appear to be actual outcrops, but may be large, loose blocks broken from outcrops high on the mountain and moved downward by landslides.

Milepost No. 329.00 Eastern end of **TANGLEFOOT CURVE.** This portion of the track is on very unstable glacial debris.

Milepost No. 330.60 **CUMBRES, COLORADO,** el. 10,015 feet. West of the station, the track leaves the glacial deposits (Qg) and returns to the chaotic, highly colored and altered volcanic breccias of the Conejos Formation (Tc). As the train slowly rounds **WINDY POINT,** M.P. 331.09, and descends into (ascends from) Wolf Creek valley, many tall spires and pinnacles are visible along the track. Another colorful display of Conejos rocks is on the high slopes to the west across Wolf Creek valley. The rocks in all these outcrops are similar to those seen at Phantom Curve and Calico Cut.

Milepost No. 332.20 **COXO, COLORADO,** el. 9,753 feet. From Coxo to Lobato Trestle, the track is on glacial and landslide debris, except for a half-mile section at Hamilton's Point. Many large, loose blocks of Conejos rocks are visible throughout the valley.

Milepost No. 332.75 Grade crossing for State Highway 17. Good views to the northwest of Windy Point and the colorful Conejos breccias.

On September 20, 1970 engine 484 was pulled dead to Chama with some of the rolling stock purchased from the Rio Grande. This photo was taken looking southeast from the hill above the grade crossing at Coxo. The rounded, hummocky slopes that are only partly tree-covered are Quaternary landslides. Small lakes, not visible from the train, fill depressions in the landslide debris.
(D. B. Osterwald)

Milepost No. 334.50 **HAMILTON'S POINT.** Between here and M.P. 334.70, the first **sedimentary** rocks not derived from volcanic sources, crop out along the track and in the cliffs across the steep canyon of Wolf Creek. These sedimentary rocks are part of the Tertiary Blanco Basin Formation (Tbb), an Oligocene (?) unit composed of material eroded from ancient highlands that were uplifted at the end of Cretaceous time. All of the material in this formation was derived from older sedimentary or Precambrian rocks; there is no known volcanic material in the Blanco Basin Formation. It is composed of white, buff, red, pink, or yellow-colored sandstones, conglomerates, and shales, containing Precambrian igneous and metamorphic rock fragments. Deposition of the Blanco Basin began at least 35 million years ago. At this locality the Formation is about 600 feet thick. On the wide, outside curve at M.P. 334.50, outcrops of the Dakota Sandstone, and of the Niobrara and Mancos Formations (Cretaceous) and the Morrison Formation (Jurassic) are visible at track level. The Morrison consists of red, green, and variegated shale and siltstone. Across the canyon is a good example of an **angular unconformity,** where the Blanco Basin Formation overlies the steeply tilted Morrison.

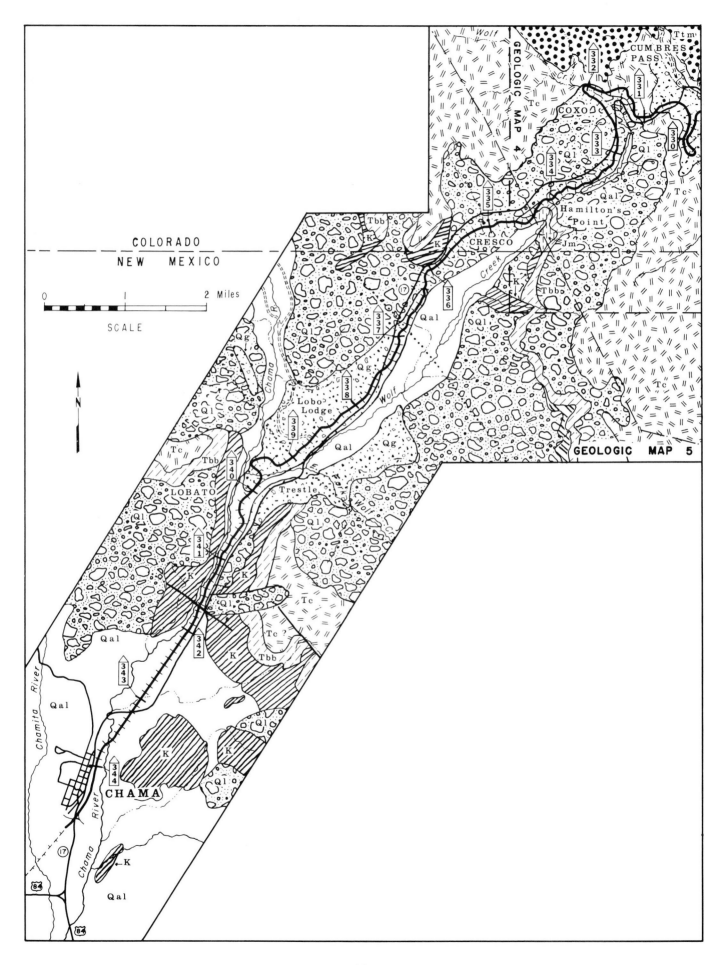

COLORADO
NEW MEXICO

0   1   2 Miles

SCALE

GEOLOGIC MAP 5

CUMBRES
PASS

COXO

CRESCO

Hamilton's
Point

Lobo
Lodge

Trestle

LOBATO

CHAMA

Milepost No. 335.10 CRESCO, COLORADO, el. 9,193 feet. This siding and water tank are built on a large landslide. Outcrops of bedrock are impossible to find here.

Milepost No. 335.60 COLORADO - NEW MEXICO state boundary for the last (first) time.

Milepost No. 336.00 Nice views of the alluvium-filled valley of Wolf Creek with large landslide scars on the upper slopes. The landslide material is younger than the glacial material, which is also present in the valley. In the highway cut above the track are outcrops of Mancos Shale. Landslides have been reactivated on the steep slope above the new highway (see p. 40).

Milepost No. 337.45 Cross State Highway 17. The railroad cuts here are in large glacial **moraines.**

Milepost No. 338.65 Grade crossing for U. S. Forest Service road to the upper Chama River valley.

Milepost No. 339.00 LOBO LODGE. From M.P. 336.20 to M.P. 340.00 the track is on morainal debris, some of which came from a glacier that moved down the Chama River valley north of Lobo Lodge, and some is from a glacier that extended down Wolf Creek valley. A veneer of morainal material lines the valley wall opposite M.P. 338.00.

The cliffs to the west are composed of the Blanco Basin Formation, beneath which are brown, resistant ledges of Dakota Sandstone. An inferred northwest-treading fault cuts through this area.

Milepost No. 339.75 LOBATO TRESTLE. Due west of the trestle, Wolf Creek joins the Chama River flowing from the north.

Milepost No. 339.99 LOBATO SIDING, cattle pens and WEED CITY. Across the Chama River the sedimentary rocks visible in the ledges are the brown to tan Dakota Sandstone at the top, and below, the variegated shales and silt-stones of the Morrison Formation. The sediments dip gently to the south.

Milepost No. 340.50 Enter (leave) the "Narrows."

Milepost No. 341.60 Across the valley to the west is a good place to see the result of movement along a fault zone. The Dakota Sandstone on the north side of the fault was dropped downward in relation to the Dakota on the south side of the fault. On the east side of the track a landslide, coming down to track level, has disrupted both the highway and the track.

Milepost No. 342.00 Leave (enter) the "Narrows." Along this straight stretch of track the 4 percent grade stops (starts). The track is built on an **outwash plain.**

Milepost No. 343.20 Grade crossing for State Highway 17.

Milepost No. 343.60 Track crosses the Chama River.

Milepost No. 344.12 CHAMA, NEW MEXICO, el. 7,863 feet, western terminus of the Cumbres and Toltec Scenic Railroad.

Across the Chama River near M.P. 341.60 is an excellent place to see faults in the Dakota Sandstone. This view west-northwest shows the Dakota down-dropped on the right side of the picture. The thickets of Gambel's oak, conifers and aspens form a dense carpet on the hills in this area. (D. B. Osterwald)

FOR THE NATURALIST

LIFE ZONES

Life zones are communities of plants and animals classified by those dominant species which thrive in a particular combination of climate and altitude. Climate is determined by both altitude and latitude. As one climbs a mountain, for every 1,000 feet rise in elevation, the average temperature drops 3° F. Put another way, climbing 2,000 feet in elevation is equivalent to traveling northward 720 miles at sea level. The Montane Zone in Colorado contains plants that are found at sea level at 50 to 60 degrees north latitude (for comparison the U. S.-Canadian border in the west is at 48 degrees north latitude). Thus desert plants do not grow and thrive in the high mountains, nor do the tiny Arctic tundra plants live in the dry climate of the plains or desert. Some plants that bloom in the San Luis Valley in June will bloom at Toltec Gorge in July or August. Animals also thrive at a particular climate and altitude. Gila monsters are never found in the Subalpine or Alpine Zones, for example.

Most classifications of life zones use trees to delineate the zone boundaries. In the Rocky Mountains of southern Colorado and northern New Mexico, 5 life zones are known: The **Plains** or **Upper Sonoran** Zone, between 3,000 and 5,500 feet; the **Foothills** or **Transition** Zone, from 5,500 to 8,000 feet; the **Montane** or **Canadian** Zone, from 8,000 to 10,000 feet; the **Subalpine** or **Hudsonian** Zone, 10,000 feet to timberline (about 12,000 feet); and the **Alpine** or **Arctic** Zone, which is above the tree line on mountain tops and has an Arctic climate.

Life zones do not have sharp boundaries, but overlap and merge into each other. Many plants are found in two or more zones. Many factors effect a plant or animal community in addition to climate and elevation. The type of soil, slope conditions, topography, moisture, humidity, wind, and temperature also effect this balance. Often one zone will be present on a north-facing slope in a valley, whereas a different zone or plant community will be found on the directly opposite south-facing slope. Some plants and animals thrive in wet, moist areas; others prefer dry, sunny slopes. Wind direction and velocity effect plant growth in many ways. Near timberline the Engelmann spruces are almost dwarfed because of the fierce winds and the high elevations. Changes from one zone to another are easier to observe in mountainous regions because of the rapid changes in altitude.

The route of the C&TS traverses the **Transition** and **Montane** Zones and touches the **Subalpine** Zone at Cumbres Pass. Some of the most common trees, shrubs, flowers, birds, and animals found in the Transition and Montane Zones listed below. A simple key for identifying some of the more common conifers is also included. A modified track profile illustrates how zones overlap.

PLANTS AND ANIMALS OF THE FOOTHILLS or TRANSITION ZONE. 5,500 to 8,000 feet elevation.

TREES: In Utah, Colorado, New Mexico, and Arizona, this zone is often referred to as the "Pinyon-Juniper Belt," as these trees are the dominant species found on the hills and in the basins between mountain ranges. At slightly higher elevations of the Pinyon-Juniper Belt, scrub oaks are common, as are the bigtooth maple and box elder; river willows and cottonwoods are along water courses. Ponderosa pine, Douglas fir, Rocky Mountain juniper, and aspen occur at the higher elevations of the Transition Zone and extend into to the Montane Zone.

SHRUBS: Mountain mahogany, rabbitbrush, squawbush, big sagebrush, cliffbush, serviceberry, chokecherry, apache plume, snowberry, barberry, and buffalo currant.

FLOWERS: Whitish blossoms: Yucca, mariposa lily, clematis, prickly poppy, foothills daisy, white sweet clover, milk vetch, horsemint, white aster, fleabane, wild onion, Rocky Mountain loco, miner's candlestick, baby aster, and Easter daisy.

Yellowish blossoms: Sweet clover, dandelion, stickweed, prickly pear cactus, oyster plant, snakeweed, goldenrod, bee plant, sunflower, golden smoke, gumweed, ragwort, sulfur flower, coneflower, and Oregon holly grape.

Pink or reddish blossoms: Buckwheat, cranesbill, loco, globemallow, cactus, pink phlox, milkweed, gilia, penstemon, and paintbrush.

Blue or purplish blossoms: Spiderwort, bee plant, milk vetch, flax, verbena, daisy, scorpionweed, tansy aster, and purple oyster plant.

BIRDS: Golden eagle, bald eagle, mourning dove, band-tailed pigeon, marsh hawk, Cooper's hawk, western red-tailed hawk, magpie, raven, red-winged blackbird, western meadowlark, grackle, pheasant, quail, Stellar's jay, pygmy nuthatch, bank swallow, black-headed grosbeak, evening grosbeak, gray-headed junco, house finch, hummingbird, and Lewis' woodpecker.

ANIMALS: Mule deer, antelope, coyote, cottontail rabbit, jackrabbit, golden-mantled ground squirrel, pine squirrel, 13-lined ground squirrel, least chipmunk, northern pocket gopher, stripped skunk, prairie dog, fox, porcupine, badger, muskrat, bat, Rocky Mountain toad, bullfrog, horned lizard, fence lizard, bullsnake, garter snake, and prairie rattlesnake.

PLANTS AND ANIMALS OF THE MONTANE ZONE. 8,000 to 10,000 feet elevation.

TREES: Thick stands of aspen, Douglas fir, lodgepole pine, white fir, limber pine, white pine, blue spruce, willow, and birch. Fewer ponderosa pine, juniper, cottonwood, and scrub oak. Engleman spruce occurs at the higher elevations, along with some subalpine fir at Cumbres and La Manga Passes.

SHRUBS: Chokecherry, ninebark, red-berried elder, mountain mahogany, squaw currant, gooseberry, apache plume, rabbitbrush, sagebrush, serviceberry, rose, raspberry.

FLOWERS: Whitish blossoms: Yucca, Canada violet, stickweed, scorpionweed, candytuft, white cranesbill, pussytoes, strawberry, gilia, phlox, wand lily, mariposa lily, miner's candlestick, yarrow, milk vetch, Rocky Mountain loco, false hellebore, thistle, buckwheat, aster, fleabane, and monument plant.

Yellowish blossoms: Oregon holly grape, draba, sage, bahia, buttercup, ox-eye daisy, golden banner, wallflower, golden smoke, puccoon, ragwort, stonecrop, cinquefoil, paintbrush, sulfur flower, sunflower, golden aster, goldenrod, butterweed, gumweed, sneezeweed, mullein, oyster plant, marsh marigold, and subalpine buttercup.

Pink or reddish blossoms: Scarlet gilia, red beardtongue, cactus, pussytoes, vetch, bearberry, locoweed, globemallow, paintbrush, cranesbill, horsemint, lousewort, fireweed, Wright's buckwheat, and scarlet penstemon.

Blue or purplish blossoms: Iris, larkspur, bull thistle, flax, chiming bell, fleabane, penstemon, lupine, loco, beard-tongue, harebell, Jacob's ladder, monkshood, aster, daisy, gentian, spiked verbena, and tansy aster.

BIRDS: Mountain bluebird, mountain chickadee, Stellar's jay, raven, Cooper's hawk, blue grouse, bald eagle, red-breasted nuthatch, house wren, tree swallow, cliff swallow, olive-sided flycatcher, Clark's nutcracker, warbling vireo, ruby-crowned kinglet, white-crowned sparrow, western tanager, pine siskin, and downy woodpecker.

ANIMALS: Mule deer, elk, coyote, bobcat, mountain lion, black bear, red fox, porcupine, Colorado chipmunk, golden-mantled ground squirrel, pine squirrel, tufted ear squirrel, Richardson's ground squirrel, muskrat, beaver, badger, otter, deer mouse, pack rat, long-tailed weasel, marten, and snowshoe rabbit.

LICHENS: Other very interesting, but very insignificant-looking plants are the **lichens.** These primitive plants are a combination of two organisms—an algae and a fungus. A green algae combines with water and sun to make food for both the algae and the fungus. The fungus absorbs and stores water, and also produces a weak acid that dissolves the rock or wood on which the lichen is growing. Lichens are among the slowest growing plants. Studies have shown that lichens grow on an average of 1 mm. to 10 mm. in radius per year. These plants can tolerate extreme drying, as the fungus protects the algae from drying out too much.

Lichens grow on rocks, trees, dead wood, mosses, and soil, and range in latitude from the hot desert to the cool tundra. These plants are very susceptible to air pollution and some species have been used to measure the degree of air pollution in our cities.

Lichens are used in antibiotics, dyes, food for animals, an emergency food for man, perfume, chemicals, and tanning leather. Some species are used for artificial trees on model railroad layouts, and in floral arrangements. Lichens help break up rocks and form soil, because the acids in the plant very slowly dissolve the cementing material and mineral grains in a rock. The wide variety of forms and colors add much interest to the appearance of rock surfaces. Many different species are abundant on the volcanic rocks along the route of the C&TS.

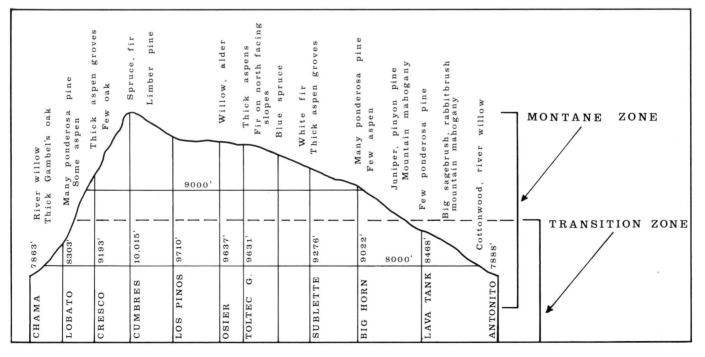

KEY TO CONIFERS

This old lithograph shows a westward view into the Conejos River valley near present-day Aspen Glade Campground. It was published in Vol. 1 of the U. S. Geographical Survey West of the 100th Meridian (Wheeler Survey Report). The drawing was probably made in 1874 as the surveying party followed the Conejos River westward. A hundred years later, aspens have hidden much of the valley floor as well as the moraines along the lower sides of the valley walls. (U. S. Geological Survey)

ENGINES

The steam locomotives (engines) at the heads of the C&TS trains are of particular interest to visitors in narrow gauge country. Three types of steam locomotives can be seen on the C&TS, although only one is in use in 1976. All three are outside-frame (K-27, K-36, K-37 series) 2-8-2[1] Mikado engines that came originally from the D&RGW; they are still numbered as they were on the Rio Grande. On outside-frame engines the drive wheels are inside the engine frames, with counterweights, side rods, and main rods connected to the ends of the axles which stick out through the frames. Outside-frame engines are heavier and more powerful than comparable-sized inside-frame types. This type of construction makes for a lot of interesting action when all the exposed machinery is in motion.

When minor repairs are completed, 463 will once more climb Cumbres Pass. The only other K-27 left is No. 464, which stood for years in the Durango yards as a neglected derelict. In November, 1973, it was sold by the Rio Grande to Knott's Berry Farm in Buena Vista, California. It has been reconditioned and is now in service. The K-27's weigh 136,650 pounds and can pull with 27,000 pounds of effort. Two of the K-27's, 455 and 461, were sold to the Rio Grande Southern Railroad and were scrapped with the rest of that road in 1952 and 1953. Two other K-27's, 458 and 459 were sold to Ferrocarrilles Nacionales de Mexico. These engines were later converted to standard gauge, and 458 was finally scrapped, but the fate of 459 is unknown. All the others were scrapped by the D&RGW.

Running gear of D&RGW engine 484 at Cumbres, Colorado, October 10, 1965. Note the counterweights, valve gear, and reverse rod. The compressed air tank is beneath the running board, behind the bank of bent cooling pipes. The three round holes between the running board and the hand rail are wash-out plugs for the boiler. The steam-driven generator (curved pipe) ahead of the cab provides electricity for the headlights, classification lights, and cab lights. (F. W. Osterwald)

The Durango roundhouse foreman contemplates the problem of rerailing 492 on July 2, 1966. The engine went on the ground after splitting a switch entering the yard. The device with large pipes just behind the running board steps is the injector, which pumps water from the tender into the boiler. Running gear of the 490's is very similar to that of the 480's. (F. W. Osterwald)

Engines of the K-27 class are almost extinct. Fifteen of these engines were built by Baldwin Locomotive Works in 1903 for the D&RG, but only two remain. No. 463 was given to the city of Antonito in 1971 by Gene Autry, who had owned it since 1955.

Three D&RGW class K-37 engines are owned by the C&TS. This class of engines, numbered in the 490 series, were the last narrow gauge engines put into service by the Rio Grande. The C&TS owns Nos. 492, 494, and 495. No. 492, although in need of inspection and repair, is in operable condition. The 494 and 495 are a convenient source of parts! The Rio Grande still owns 491, 493, 497, 498, and 499; 490 and 496 were scrapped. The 490's had checkered careers—they were originally built in 1902 by Baldwin as standard gauge 2-8-0's (D&RG class C-41).

[1]The Whyte system of classifying steam locomotives, as used in the United States, describes the wheel arrangement. Thus a 2-8-2 engine has 2 non-powered pilot wheels in front, 8 powered drive wheels, and 2 non-powered trailing wheels in addition to the tender wheels.

In 1928 and 1930, 10 of the C-41 engines were rebuilt in Denver at the Burnham Shops of the D&RGW as narrow gauge 2-8-2's. When rebuilt, the engines weighed 307,250 pounds with their loaded tenders, and could pull with 37,100 pounds of effort. The 490-series engines had a reputation for being "stiff" and subject to derailments. Look under the tender on a 490 at Antonito or Chama to see evidence of their history—the tender wheels were simply shoved closer together to fit narrow gauge track, using the original axles and truck side-frames.

The real workers of the C&TS are the 480-series engines (D&RGW K-36 Class). The Colorado-New Mexico Railroad Authorities own Nos. 482, 483, 484, 487, 488, and 489. The 482 and 489 are the only ones not operable. Ten of these locomotives were built by Baldwin for the Rio Grande in 1925; these were the last new narrow gauge engines acquired by the Rio Grande, and were a part of the general upgrading and rebuilding of narrow gauge routes during the 1920's. No. 485 was scrapped before the C&TS was formed. The 480 is presently (1976) stored in poor condition at Alamosa. The 481 in 1976 is still owned by the D&RGW, and is stored in operating condition at Durango. This engine, after a major overhaul at Alamosa, was hauled west in the last Rio Grande freight over Cumbres in 1968. No. 486 is on display at the Royal Gorge near Canon City, Colorado. These engines weigh 286,000 pounds with their loaded tenders, and can pull with 36,200 pounds of effort. The tenders carry 9.5 tons of coal and 5,000 gallons of water.

The K-36 engines have had a colorful history. In addition to their normal freight-hauling duties, they frequently pulled the deluxe "San Juan" daily passenger train from Alamosa to Durango. In this role, they substituted for the 470 engines, now used on the D&RGW's Silverton Branch. In 1941, Forrest Crosson, riding one of the last trains to Santa Fe, New Mexico, wrote a very notable description of engine 483 pulling the train from Alamosa to Antonito, meeting a 470-series engine that took the Santa Fe-bound cars southward from Antonito. The 483 then went westward with the "San Juan" to Chama and Durango. The 483 also worked on the Marshall Pass, Colorado line between Salida and Gunnison shortly before this route was abandoned, and has hauled many cars of limestone down the Monarch Pass, Colorado branch before that track was standard-gauged and dieselized in 1956. The engine on the last eastbound special passenger train from Durango to Alamosa in November 1968 was 483. The 483 was then used as the helper to Cumbres on the last westbound D&RGW train to Durango. It was next used to power the first C&TS work trains during the volunteer operations to re-open the track from Antonito to Chama in 1970. The 483 was the only engine available for this work, still wearing its colorful 1968 red, brown and gold paint job for the movie, "The Good Guys and the Bad Guys," filmed near Chama. All was not glamour for 483, however, as she turned over near Durango, Colorado in 1958, killing the fireman.

Engine 483 ready for the pass. Chama roundhouse, 1939. The large collection of tanks and pipes on the side above the fourth driver is a steam-driven cross-compound pump, providing compressed air for the brakes. This pump makes a characteristic ka-thunk, ka-thunk sound when the engine is stopped while under steam. The brakeman's doghouse was removed from the tender for a movie in 1968; in 1975 it was beside the D&RGW roundhouse in Durango. (Turner Van Nort)

Engine 484 also worked on the "San Juan" as well as on freights. The 484 was the helper engine to Cumbres on the last eastbound "San Juan" on January 31, 1951, having been the road engine from Durango to Chama. After the abandonment of the "San Juan" in 1951, 484 sometimes pulled a one-car passenger train from Chama westward to Dulce, New Mexico. The consist of this train was combination car 212, now a regular fixture on the Silverton Branch.

The last chartered D&RGW excursion train from Alamosa to Cumbres and return, October 9, 1966, was pulled by 484, as was the first C&TS revenue train on June 26, 1971. Other 480's also took part in notable events on the narrow gauge, some of which were sad for railroaders. Number 482 pulled the last regular train northward through the San Luis Valley, Colorado, from Alamosa to Salida. No. 488 was the road engine on the last "San Juan" from Chama to Alamosa. No. 489 was a helper engine on the last revenue train over Marshall Pass ,Colorado, from Salida to Gunnison, and also pulled the scrap train on Marshall Pass after abandonment.

One prominent feature of the Chama yards is engine 19, which is a 44-ton General Electric diesel-electric, owned by Scenic Railways, Inc., that was purchased in 1972 from the Oahu Railway in Hawaii. Affectionately known as "The Pineapple," 19 is used in switching, work train duties, and for occasional passenger runs originating from Cumbres. During shipment to Chama, it was discovered that "The Pineapple" actually weighs 47 tons—three tons of concrete ballast were added by the Oahu Railway to increase the traction!

Two other small steam engines may be seen at Chama; No. 5 is in operating condition and was used briefly on a tourist line in California, and another, No. 13 is presently disassembled. Both were obtained in Hawaii, and are owned by Scenic Railways, Inc. A

small wooden caboose, a relic from the Westside Lumber Company narrow gauge railroad in California, is privately owned.

CARS

The passenger cars of the C&TS are converted from D&RGW 3000 series boxcars. Twenty-six of these 30-foot boxcars were purchased from the Rio Grande by the Colorado and New Mexico Railroad Authorities; a few additional ones were purchased later by Scenic Railways, Inc. for use on the C&TS. These boxcars were originally built during 1903 and 1904 for the D&RG. During various modifications and rebuildings, modern couplers and air brake equipment were added. During a major rebuilding in 1924-26, the cars received metal roofs. As rebuilt the cars could carry 50,000 pounds; they weigh 22,700 pounds empty.

The first C&TS passenger car, number 200, was constructed from boxcar 3339 in 1971, by volunteer workers. The original paint on No. 200 was red with gold lettering and striping. The seats were length-wise in the center, facing outward, but the steps and windows provided the prototype for all the other cars used in 1976. Several other boxcars were converted rapidly for the 1971 passenger season.

Only one caboose, No. 0503, was included in the sale of equipment to the Railroad Authorities. The caboose was built in 1880 by the D&RG, and rebuilt with modern couplers and air-brake equipment in 1923. No marker lights were delivered with the caboose, so it is operated with borrowed markers or with red flags on the rear end.

Among the heaviest cars on the C&TS are the 14 6500-series steel frame flatcars, 41 feet 6 inches long, that can carry as much as 107,700 pounds. They were rebuilt from standard gauge flatcars by the Rio Grande between 1940 and 1944. One of their most

Flat cars loaded with new automobiles, D&RGW yard, Durango, Colorado, September, 1951. (F. W. Osterwald)

notable uses was to carry new automobiles to Durango, and to other towns west of Durango on the Rio Grande Southern Railroad. For this purpose the flatcars were equipped with canvas covers over a lightweight steel framework. Other flatcars in the 6600-series were converted from standard gauge stock and boxcars in 1955 by the Rio Grande at Pueblo, Colorado. The 6700-series flatcars were converted from narrow gauge box or stock cars in 1957, and were used mainly as idler cars in trains of oil and gas field pipe destined for Farmington, New Mexico. An idler flat was coupled to each end of an open-end high-side gondola car loaded with pipes or long poles which extended beyond both ends of the gondola. This allowed the long pipe sections to be carried around the crooked track from Antonito to Chama. In the late 1950's, more than 6,000 carloads of pipe were carried from Alamosa to Farmington annually, totaling more than 100,000 tons.

Examples of several types of gondola cars can be seen in the C&TS yards. The oldest gondolas are the 9500-series, built between 1898 and 1902. The 1000-series were built between 1902 and 1904. The 700- and 800-series drop-bottom gondolas, built in 1904, are used occasionally to carry track ballast or other materials on work trains. The 43-foot long, 9600-series open-end gondolas, are the longest cars on the C&TS and were rebuilt from standard gauge boxcars in 1953 to haul pipe. These cars can carry a maximum load of 106,400 pounds. All gondolas except the 9600-series carried maximum loads of 55,000 pounds.

Perhaps the most interesting cars on the C&TS are the various types of work equipment. Foremost among these are the two rotary snowplows, OM at Chama, and OY at Antonito. The rotors in the fronts of these plows are driven by steam, from boilers connected to flywheels inside the plow bodies. Chutes at the top of the rotor housings direct the plowed snow to either side of the track. The OM was built in 1889 by the Cooke Locomotive Works. The gabled roof over the tender and the cab roof and side extensions on OM were added by the D&RGW to keep snow out of the coal and off the fireman. Rotary OY was built in 1923. In operation, rotary plows are pushed by one or more locomotives. They require crews of at least three; a **pilot** (qualified locomotive engineer) to coordinate forward movement of the plow and its locomotives, a **wheelman** (also a qualified locomotive engineer) to control the direction of the snow deflector, and a **fireman,** in addition to the crews on the locomotives. Rotary trains are run occasionally on the C&TS in winter, for the benefit of interested railroad fans and photographers. It's a great sight and lots of fun.

One may see a large red steel passenger coach either in the yards or on special trains. This coach was bought in Mexico by the Rio Grande and San Juan Railroad Company, probably from the Nacionales de Mexico, and presumably for use on excursion trains over Cumbres. It was renamed the **Arthur Ridgway,** and sat in the Rio Grande yards in Alamosa from 1967 to 1971. The owner, Thomas J. Hinman, loaned it to the C&TS in 1971, and after being placed on U.S. narrow gauge freight trucks (Mexican narrow gauge trucks are higher than those used in the U.S.) it was moved to Chama. It is used occasionally for special trains and for movies, and played starring roles in "Showdown" and "Bite the Bullet."

TRACK

The Cumbres and Toltec Scenic Railroad is narrow gauge. It was built that way by the Denver & Rio Grande, whose officials knew that a narrow gauge road could be built and operated more cheaply than one built to standard gauge. "Narrow gauge" simply means that the inside surfaces of the rails (and

Switching a train fo pipe, south end fo Chama yards, June, 1953. Trainman at left end or right gondola is giving hand signal directions to the engineer.

(F. W. Osterwald)

Engine 483 at the stone D&RGW depot in Antonito, Colorado with the last passenger train operated by the Rio Grande over Cumbres Pass. This train was provided for a two-day inspection trip from Durango for members of the National Park Service, the press, Rio Grande officials, and other individuals interested in preserving at least a part of the narrow gauge between Antonito and Durango. The dual gauge (3 rail) track for the San Juan Division ends a short distance west of the depot. The southbound standard gauge track ends at the perlite plants in the middle distance below San Antonio Peak on the skyline. November, 1968. (Ernest W. Robart)

the outer surfaces of the wheel flanges on the locomotives and cars) are less than 4 feet 8½ inches apart. Exactly why a gauge of 4 feet 8½ inches was adopted as standard in Britain and North America is not known, but perhaps coincidentally, this distance is the same as the distance between the wheels of Roman chariots. Most narrow gauge railroads in the U.S., including the D&RG, were built with rails 3 feet apart, but many used 2-foot or 3½-foot gauge track. The Colorado-New Mexico area formerly contained hundreds of miles of narrow gauge track, mostly of 3-foot gauge, although there were several notable 2-foot gauge lines and a few of 3½-foot gauge.

Because the original narrow gauge engines and cars were smaller and lighter than standard gauge equipment, they could be operated safely on lighter rails and over less sturdily constructed bridges than could standard gauge equipment. Most narrow gauge equipment, being short, can operate around sharper curves than can standard gauge trains. Unfortunately, however, for most narrow gauges, light rail and sharp curves limit the speed of trains. Slow schedules and the expense of transferring freight to standard gauge cars have caused nearly all narrow gauges in the U. S. to disappear. Only the D&RGW Silverton Branch, the White Pass and Yukon Railroad in Alaska, and the C&TS survive as common carriers. (The C&TS does occasionally carry freight.) Of these, only the

Westbound D&RGW engines #473 and #483 arriving in Antonito with the last freight train ever operated by the Rio Grande over Cumbres Pass to Durango. Recently overhauled engine 481 was included in the consist, as it was being transported dead for possible use on the "Silverton." December 5, 1968.

Ernest W. Robart

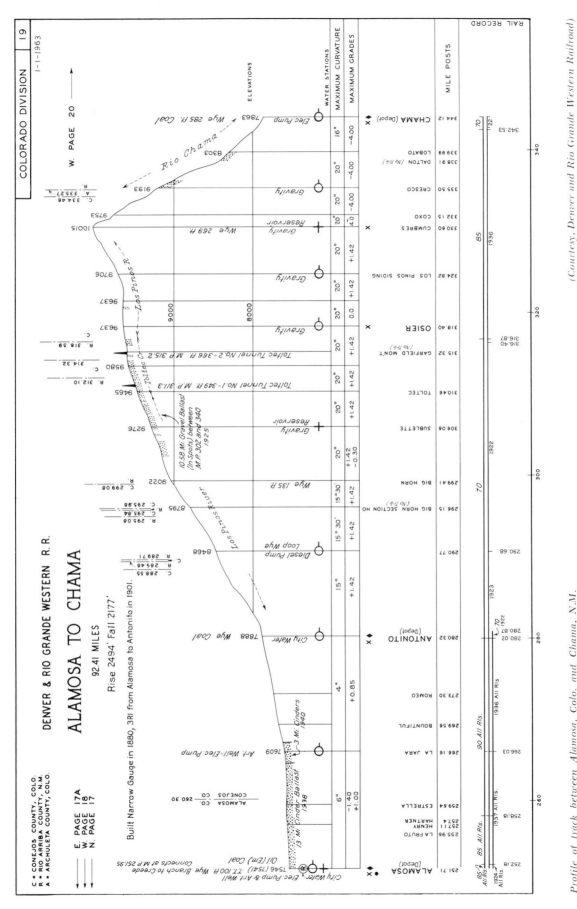

DENVER & RIO GRANDE WESTERN R. R.

ALAMOSA TO CHAMA

92.41 MILES

Rise 2494' Fall 2177'

Built Narrow Gauge in 1880, 3Ri from Alamosa to Antonito in 1901.

(Courtesy, Denver and Rio Grande Western Railroad)

Profile of track between Alamosa, Colo. and Chama, N.M.

WP&Y regularly operates both passenger and freight trains, the freight traffic surviving beause there is no need for interchange with a standard gauge road.

Interchange expenses caused the D&RG to standard gauge most of the original narrow gauge main lines. Two notable exceptions were the original Denver to Ogden, Utah main line via Pueblo, Salida, Gunnison, and Grand Junction, Colorado, and the San Juan Extension to Durango and Silverton, Colorado. As more of the track became standard gauge, the interchange point retreated from Denver southward to Pueblo, Salida, and Walsenburg, reaching Alamosa in 1899. Standard gauge rails reached Antonito, Colorado in 1901, but were operated mostly by narrow gauge engines on 3-rail track, using special idler cars carrying additional couplers on each end to fit cars of both gauges. One of the idler cars, although mounted on standard gauge trucks, is owned by the CT&S and can be seen in the Chama yards, loaded on a narrow gauge flatcar. The interchange point between narrow gauge and standard gauge remained in Alamosa until the D&RGW abandoned the narrow gauge in 1970.

Dual gauge idler car derailed in the Alamosa yards, June 11, 1967.
(Ed Osterwald)

The original track over Cumbres was laid with very light 30-pound iron rail (rail weights are given in pounds per yard of rail length, so 30-pound rail weighs 30 pounds per yard). The source of this rail is not known, but it probably came from mills in the eastern U. S. or from England. The first rails rolled at the D&RG-controlled Colorado Coal and Iron Company in Pueblo were hauled over Cumbres in 1882 for use between Durango and Silverton. Rails weighing 40 and 45 pounds per yard made up most of the track from Alamosa to Durango by 1913. These rails were strong enough to support the small 2-8-0 and 4-6-0 engines then in common use. Heavier 2-8-2, K-27

engines had been in use westward from Salida to Gunnison since 1903, but could not be used on Cumbres at that time because of the light rail. In 1913, 14½ miles of track from Chama to Cumbres were relaid with used 65-pound steel rail. The 2-8-2 engines could then be used as helpers on the steep grade to Cumbres, although they had to be hauled unloaded to Chama before they could be placed in service. These engines were too heavy for the 40-pound rails when fully loaded. Seventy-pound rails were laid from Antonito to M.P. 316 (about 1½ miles east of Osier), and from Chama eastward for about 1½ miles in 1922 and 1923. In 1936, 85-pound rails were laid from M.P. 316 to the point 1½ miles east of Chama, permitting the heaviest classes of D&RGW narrow gauge engines (ie., K-36 and K-37) to be used on both sides of the Cumbres Pass.

The C&TS track is very steep from Chama to Cumbres, with a maximum grade of 4 per cent, meaning that the track rises 4 feet for every 100 feet along the track. The grade is not a constant 4 per cent, however, as shown by the profile, page 70. From Antonito to Cumbres the grade is much less steep, averaging about 0.8 per cent, attaining in places a maximum of 1.42 per cent. Some track is nearly level for short distances.

Railroad curves are measured in **degrees,** describing the angle marked at the center of the curve by two radial lines drawn from the ends of a 100-foot long chord to the curve. Maximum curvature on the C&TS is 20 degrees between Big Horn Wye and Lobato. Many sharp curves on both sides of Cumbres have additional rails spiked inside the running rails. These are guard rails designed to keep car wheels close to the running rails in case of derailment.

The D&RG, at several times, planned to standard gauge the Cumbres route. One of the most obvious indications of such intent was the track between Durango, Colorado, and Farmington, New Mexico, which was originally built to standard gauge, and later converted to narrow gauge. Other indications are the large steel bridges at Lobato and Cascade Creek, which were built to standard gauge specifications. Anticipated widening of gauge resulted in widened fills near Sublette, and occasional sections in which standard gauge ties were installed.

The bridges at Cascade Creek and Lobato have involved histories. The original bridge at Cascade Creek was a 27-panel wooden trestle, 432 feet long and 116 feet high, with 28 bents. According to Jackson C. Thode, of the D&RGW, an iron bridge with bents about 80 feet high, and a deck composed of girders 54 feet and 30 feet long, was purchased and delivered in 1880. In 1886, the girders were taken out and installed as common deck girder bridges elsewhere on the system; 5 going to the First Division between Denver and Palmer Lake, Colorado, and 3 to the Third Division (Marshall Pass). The First Division bridges were too light for heavy engines, and were returned to Cascade in 1889. Two new 54-foot and one new 30-foot girders were ordered for Cascade Trestle in 1888, probably to replace the portions sent to Marshall Pass.

Narrow gauge engine 497 switching a standard gauge train at the perlite plant south of Antonito, June, 1953. A dual gauge idler car is the first car behind the engine tender.
(F. W. Osterwald)

Lobato trestle, M.P. 339.75. This short, eastbound C&TS extra was chartered by a liquor company in June, 1973. The consist and train crew were photographed by an advertising company at several localities along the route. The hand-rail and walk-way were added to the bridge in 1945. Note the absence of longitudinal bracing.
(Ed Osterwald)

The Lobato trestle apparently was originally iron, as Ernest Ingersoll described crossing "a lofty iron bridge" near Lobato in his account copyrighted in 1885. This trestle, and the iron bridge at Cascade, were of an innovative German design using doubly tapered bents requiring no cross-bracing. The present steel bridges also have tapered bents.

TERMINALS AND FACILITIES

One of the concepts upon which the purchase of the track and equipment by the Colorado and New Mexico Railroad Authorities was based, was that it could provide an operating museum of narrow gauge mountain railroading. The Chama terminal fits this concept well, because all of the structures date from the period of D&RGW mainline operation. The Chama terminal was a busy place during mainline operations, because Chama was a point where engines and crews were changed. Chama also was a helper station where as many as 400 engine servicings were done monthly during the oil boom of the 1950's. Several trains passed through Chama every day.

The original 6-stall, wooden roundhouse at Chama was built in 1882, and burned in 1899, (this apparently was a common fate for many early roundhouses). The present brick roundhouse originally had 9 stalls. Four stalls were removed by the D&RGW in 1936, and 3 more disappeared in the early 1950's. East of the roundhouse was a large plant built in 1900 for dipping sheep in chemicals to kill ticks and other pests—the track which led to this plant is still in place. The original roundhouse had a 50-foot Keystone turntable; this was replaced by a 65-foot turntable in 1925 to handle larger helper engines.

Another prominent feature of the Chama yards is the coal tower. This structure was built in 1924, replacing a 60-ton coal chute built in 1902. It was originally painted a red color similar to that used on boxcars—the red paint can still be seen under the accumulation of coal dust. The tower may also be the only operating coaling tower for steam locomotives left in the U. S. The water tank was built in 1897, and may be the only operable double-spout tank left in the U.S.

A track scale, apparently obtained second hand from Aspen, Colorado, was installed in 1889. It was replaced by a larger track scale in 1929, which is still in place.

The original Chama depot, built in 1882, burned in 1899. It was replaced by the existing depot the same year. The Chama depot was painted white with dark green trim during the last years of the D&RGW operation, as were other small buildings. The brick oil house, office and storeroom were built in 1903. The original color schemes used in Chama are not known. The section house, now used as housing for volunteer railroaders, is a classic example of rough-hewn solid log construction. An almost identical building stands at Sublette. A prominent feature of the Chama yards is the stockyards, located on the tail of the wye near the south end of the yards. These stockyards were built in 1888, and were enlarged in 1915.

Except for an unused sheet-metal covered warehouse, which was removed to make room for a passengers' parking lot, and for the removal of the freight and express dock from the depot, the Chama terminal looks very much as it did during D&RGW ownership.

The original D&RG depot (probably wooden) at Antonito was built in 1880 near the junction of the tracks to Santa Fe, New Mexico and to Durango, Colorado. This building was soon converted to a freight house, and a stone depot was built 116 feet north of the wooden depot, adjacent to the switch for the San Juan Extension. A 3-room addition was built onto the stone depot in 1917. The building is still in use by the D&RGW, as the sale to the states did not include the Antonito yards, depot, or wye. This caused many problems for the early operation of the C&TS because engine 483 had to be turned at Lava or Big Horn, and run in reverse all the way to Antonito. Coal-loading facilities for the D&RG at Antonito originally consisted of a coal dock, built in 1888. A new coal chute was built in 1909. This chute was replaced by a functional, but less picturesque, coal-loader in 1956. A one-stall engine house long enough for two **small** engines, was built in 1883 directly across the track from the depot at Antonito, primarily to service engines on the Santa Fe branch of the D&RGW. This engine house was retired in 1927 and is not the present structure seen near the C&TS depot.

The C&TS depot, tool shed, yards, engine house, and turning facilities have been constructed since 1970 by either the Colorado-New Mexico Railroad Authorities, or by Scenic Railways, Inc. The new engine house was built by the people of Antonito with donations and a financial grant. Engine 463 is being repaired (1976) in this building.

Other notable structures and facilities between Antonito and Chama are described in the mile by mile guide. Because of its strategic location, Cumbres was an important station throughout the period of the Rio Grande operation. Helper engines were turned and

Chama, New Mexico, June 1953, a busy year for the Rio Grande. These engines are ready for a "hill turn." The roundhouse which once had 9 stalls had 5 stalls at the time this photo was taken.
(F. W. Osterwald)

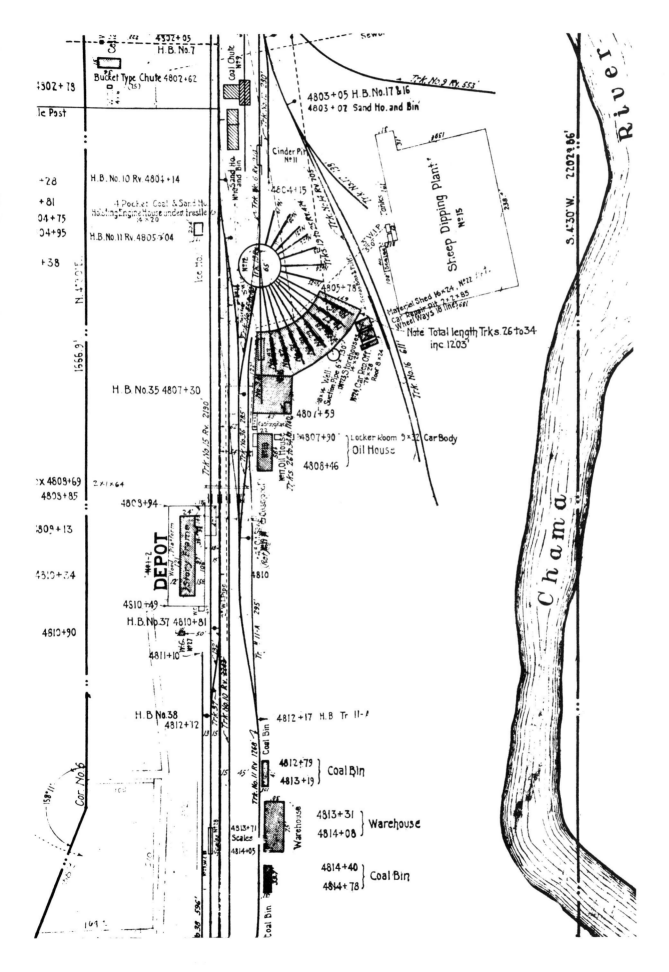

Right of way and track map of Chama, New Mexico, corrected to December 31, 1936.

(Courtesy Denver and Rio Grande Western Railroad)

In 1939 the 65-foot turntable north of the Chama roundhouse was still in use. The bent steel rod below the engine cylinders and in front of the first two drivers was used to push the table around by hand. The table had wheels at each end which ran on a circle of rail in the bottom of the pit (visible at bottom of picture below the cylinder heads). The ash pit at the right edge of the picture, behind the tender, is still in place. Engine 480 is still on the D&RGW roster.

(Turner Van Nort)

serviced there, as they are now, for both eastbound and westbound trains. About 3000 feet of sidings are at Cumbres. The yards were used for inspection and storage of cars as eastbound trains were reassembled to continue their trips after being brought from Chama in several "cuts." An agent and a section foreman were stationed at Cumbres early in the history of the railroad. A car repairer also was stationed there in the early 1900's.

A 1½ story 24-foot by 38-foot frame depot was built at Cumbres in 1882; it was removed during the winter of 1953-4. The present Cumbres depot was the original section house, also built in 1882. The station signal on the present depot-section house was built by volunteers in 1972 to duplicate a D&RGW design that was installed on the original depot in 1888. A bunk house for section men was also built in 1882. The car repairer's house, a rather ramshackle building still standing north of the depot-section house, was built in 1911.

To service engines, Cumbres also had a 50-foot covered gallows turntable that was installed in 1884, in addition to the still existing snowshed-covered wye. The turntable probably was moved to Monarch, Colorado, but the date is unknown. A coal platform was built in 1888, and is probably the one still existing at the west leg of the covered wye. A sandhouse existed for a time, but no data is available on it. Water for locomotives at Cumbres has been obtained from a nat-

ural lake north of the wye since 1880. For a time, water was pumped to a tank by a windmill, and later by a gasoline engine. The tank was replaced by the present cistern and water plug at some unknown time.

OPERATION

The San Juan Extension probably became the San Juan Division after completion of the line to Silverton in 1881. Later the Cumbres Pass route became part of the Second Division of the D&RG Railway Co., which extended from La Veta, Colorado to Silverton. In a general renumbering of divisions in 1888, Cumbres Pass became part of the Fourth Division.

Normal operation of the Cumbres Pass route by the D&RGW definitely had a mainline flavor. In addition to a daily passenger train each way, there was at least one daily freight in each direction. Nor were these freights small affairs. Fifty- to 70-car trains were common in the 1950's. Occasional trains of more than 100 cars wormed their way down to Antonito from the pass. In 1955 about 12,000 car loads of freight were handled to or from the Chama-Durango-Farmington area. Two, three and four engines were used on many eastbound trains.

Schedules were never particularly fast. In 1881, westbound passenger trains were scheduled to leave Antonito at 7 A.M. and to arrive in Chama at 1 P.M. A freight train was scheduled to leave Antonito at 8 A.M. and to reach Chama at 4 P.M.

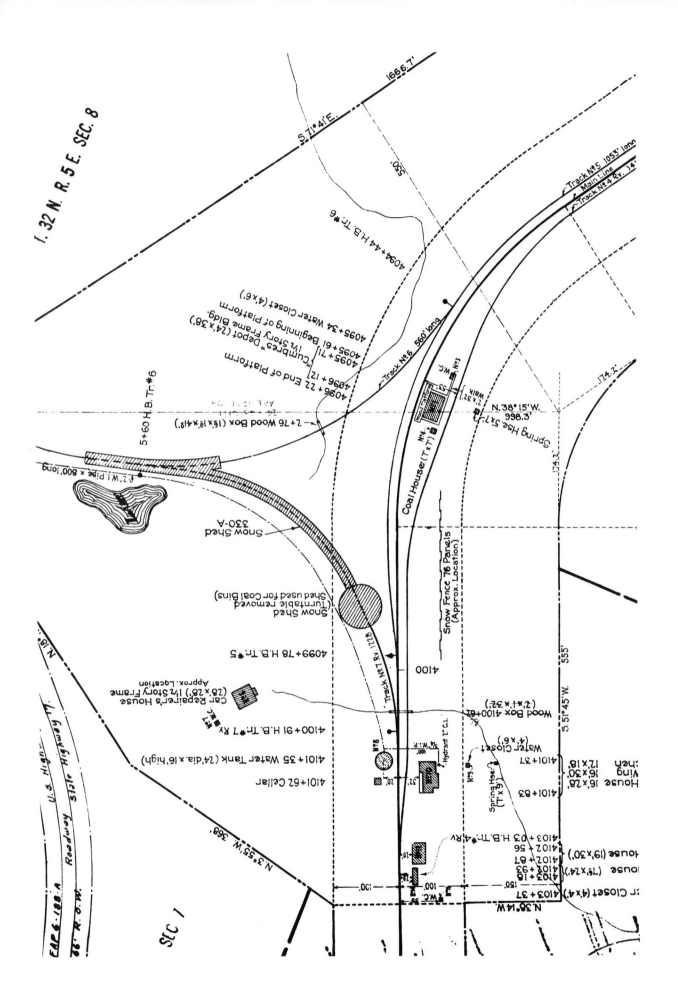

Right of way and track map of Cumbres, Colorado, corrected to December 31, 1936.

(Courtesy Denver and Rio Grande Western Railroad)

Engines 493 and 497 with a "Cumbres turn" at Coxo, August 29, 1967. This is the crossing on old State Highway 17, a favorite photo spot of many railfans.

(R. W. Osterwald)

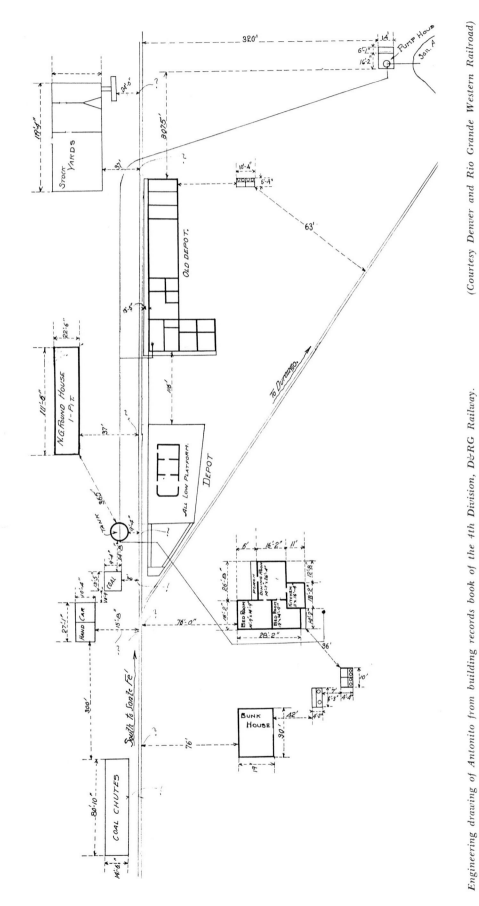

Engineering drawing of Antonito from building records book of the 4th Division, D&RG Railway.

(*Courtesy Denver and Rio Grande Western Railroad*)

Coal chute at Antonito in about 1902. Engineer Jack Law shoved a little too hard with his 160 engine! It was easier to dismantle the car in place than to get it down in one piece.

(W. D. Joyce collection)

C&TS rotary OM plowing in the "narrows" in February, 1975. Note the rotor blades and the chute (behind the headlight). The tender used on OM came from 2-8-2 engine No. 30 of the Uintah Railway, in northwestern Colorado and eastern Utah.

(Becky Osterwald)

Schedules in 1894 were a little faster; the passenger train left Antonito at 11:20 A.M. and arrived in Chama at 2:55 P.M. In its later years, however, the "San Juan" left Antonito at 8:15 A.M. and arrived at Chama at about noon. Your trip on the C&TS really isn't much slower than a ride on the "San Juan," if time for photo runs and lunch is excluded. During snow blockades, however, D&RGW trains were weeks late.

Eastward Rio Grande freights from Chama required special operations. Two K-36 or K-37 engines could handle from 12 to 15 loaded cars up the 4 percent grade. Trains were cut into several parts, and each part was taken to Cumbres separately. The road engine was in front, with a helper at the rear. At Cumbres the cars were set out in the yards and the engines turned on the wye, so they could return to Chama for another "hill turn." When all the cuts were hauled to Cumbres, the train was reassembled. Westbound freights presented problems too. At Antonito a helper engine was placed in the middle of the train. If the train was very long, or heavy, an additional engine was coupled ahead of the road engine, and perhaps a fourth added to the rear, ahead of the caboose.

Double-headed trains have their difficulties either eastbound or westbound. Weight restrictions require that at least five cars be placed between engines crossing the bridges at Lobato and Cascade Creek. That is why, if one is lucky enough to ride a double-headed C&TS train, a stop will be made at Lobato, and the helper will be cut off to cross the bridge light. The rest of the train then follows and rejoins the helper on the opposite side of the bridge.

The popular concept of pioneer Western railroads

hauling solid trainloads of ore is not wholly correct for the Cumbres line. Although originally built to reach metal mining districts in the San Juan Mountains, most of the traffic consisted of mining machinery, supplies, household goods, food, coal, lumber, and other mining-related commodities. Most of the ore, however, was milled and smelted near the mines, at Silverton and Durango, so only refined metal or mill concentrates were shipped over Cumbres Pass. Large numbers of livestock were shipped as ranching developed in the areas served by the D&RG. Large stands of timber south and west of Chama provided enormous quantities of lumber which went eastward over Cumbres. During the 1940's, many carloads of pinto beans came from farming areas west of Durango. Fruit came from Farmington. Although not as glamorous as gold and silver, prosaic agricultural products probably accounted for much more traffic than mining.

The Farmington (San Juan Basin) oil boom during the 1950's furnished the last traffic bonanza. In addition to solid trains of pipe, large amounts of drilling mud, oilfield machinery, and supplies were delivered via the Cumbres narrow gauge track. Crude oil was shipped from Chama eastward to a refinery at Alamosa. Oil gave the narrow gauge one of its most characteristic features—privately owned tank cars labeled simply "GRAMPS" in large letters. The owner of the oilfield is reported to have asked his grandchildren how they thought the cars should be marked!

The narrow gauge 2-8-2 engines make as much noise, smoke and steam as medium-sized standard gauge engines, and the whistles are just as loud. The nickname "The Little Train," sometimes applied to the C&TS, simply does not fit.

GRAMPS tank car in Antonito yards, June, 1953. The GRAMPS herald was white; reporting marks were yellow. These cars had no underframes. (F. W. Osterwald)

Narrow gauge steel-frame tank cars standing in the Chama yards, 1939. The oil-loading rack is at left of picture behind the GRAMPS tank. UTLX cars were black with yellow lettering. (Turner Van Nort)

Train load of oil field pipe in Alamosa yards ready to leave for Farmington, N. M., May, 1968. (F. W. Osterwald)

Retainer valve on narrow gauge flat car, Alamosa yards, May, 1969. Moving the handle to the 10 lbs. or 20 lbs. position reduces the air pressure in the brake system on the car so that only 10 or 20 pounds per square inch pressure is maintained.
(F. W. Osterwald)

D&RG rotary plow OM working east of Cumbres, probably in March, 1909. Compare the small tender and large oil headlight on OM with the picture of the C&TS rotary on page 79. Engine 203 also has a large oil headlight, a diamond stack, and ornate fluted domes not found on more modern equipment. Monte Ballough photo.   *(Jackson C. Thode collection)*

Rio Grande Southern rotary plow No. 2 near Cumbres on a rare trip to help the D&RG clear a snow blockade in February, 1900. Monte Ballough photo.   *(Jackson C. Thode collection)*

D&RG rotary plow OM working eastward up the 4 percent below Hamilton's Point, powered by 4 small engines, probably in 1900. Monte Ballough photo. (*Jackson C. Thode collection*)

Ex-D&RGW rotary plow OY at Antonito, 1973. This plow which is larger and newer than OM, was overhauled at the Rio Grande's Alamosa shops before abandonment, but not used before its purchase for the C&TS. Note the Fox-patent trucks. The small spoked wheels below the rotor housing are on a motor-car trailer. (*C. R. Osterwald*)

ROLLING STOCK

Taking water at Chama, August 29, 1967.   *(C. R. Osterwald)*

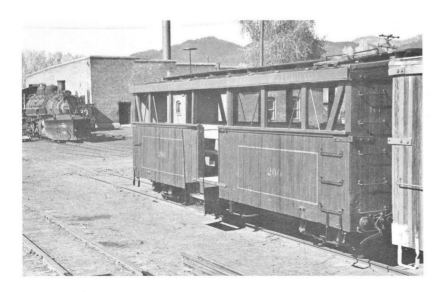

The first C&TS passenger car, No. 200, was built with volunteer labor in the spring of 1971. This car was painted brighter red than the D&RGW boxcars, and had gold lettering and striping.

(D. B. Osterwald)

End details of 3000-series D&RGW boxcar at Durango, Colo., June, 1966. (*F. W. Osterwald*)

Ex-D&RGW 3000-series boxcar nearly converted to C&TS coach No. 204, Chama, N.M., June, 1971. (*Ed Osterwald*)

Boxcars of the 3000-series at Farmington, N. M., July, 1972. Note the details of steps, grab irons, corner-braces, and door latches. Roofs were metal-sheathed.

(*Ed Osterwald*)

Lettering and detail placement on side of D&RGW 3000-series boxcar at A end, Alamosa, Colo., May, 1968.

(F. W. Osterwald)

Lettering placement and door details, B end of D&RGW boxcar 3477, Alamosa, Colo., May, 1968.

(F. W. Osterwald)

D&RGW long refrigerator car in Antonito yards after eastbound trip over Cumbres, June, 1952. "Reefer" is coupled between a GRAMPS tank car and boxcar 3311. Note truss rods and Andrews trucks on reefer, as well as the arrangement of door hinges, latch bars, grab irons, ladders, and ice-hatch lift bars. Narrow gauge D&RGW reefers were "reefer yellow" with black lettering and oxide red ends and roofs. (F. W. Osterwald)

Narrow-gauge short reefers after overhaul and new paint jobs at Alamosa shops in 1940. None of these cars remain in operating condition. (Turner Van Nort)

Three-quarter side view of drop-bottom gondola 731 in Alamosa, May 5, 1968, showing drop mechanism, bottom doors, grab irons, coupler lift bay, and corner bracing, and placement of brake wheel and retainer valve. Pipe-like object beside brake wheel is a stack on a structure behind the car. (Ed Osterwald)

Three-quarter front view of B-end of drop-bottom gondola 836, isolated at Arboles, Colo., July, 1971. Note arrangement of grab irons, handles to drop the bottom, coupler lift mechanism, corner bracing, and bolt arrangement. (Ed Osterwald)

Three-quarter end view of D&RGW double-deck stock car No. 5713 in Chama, N. M. yards, June 12, 1967. Note grab irons, end bracing, poling pockets, truss rods, and arch bar trucks. These cars were black with white lettering. (Ed Osterwald)

Stock cars 5807 and 5559 with two decks, used for hauling sheep. Alamosa yards, 1940.   (*Turner Van Nort*)

Side-view of drop-bottom gondola 837 showing truck side-frames, truss-rods, and dump mechanism. June 13, 1967.

(*Ed Osterwald*)

D&RGW high-side gondola 9243 in yard at Durango, Colo., Sept., 1951. Note arch-bar trucks, truss-rods, arrangement of side-braces, and brake wheel. D&RGW narrow gauge couplers are the same size as standard gauge couplers. All D&RGW narrow gauge revenue freight equipment, except reefers, tank cars, and stock cars, was painted oxide red with white lettering. (F. W. Osterwald)

D&RGW open-end high-side gondola on an isolated piece of track at Gato, Colo., July, 1971. Observe placements of brake wheel, grab irons and side braces. End sill detail includes truss-rod ends, as well as a coupler and draft gear details. (Ed Osterwald)

B-end of D&RGW high-side gondola, C&TS yards, Antonito, showing arrangement of grab-irons and coupler lift bar. June 26, 9171. (Ed Osterwald)

Narrow gauge Jordan spreader OU, used for ballasting track, scraping back loose cuts, and plowing snow when coupled behind a flanger. Air pressure actuates arms which move the large blades forward. Large tank is air reservoir; operator stands in the small shelter. Note arch-bar trucks, brake wheel placement and end-sill detail. All work equipment is painted gray with black lettering. May, 1968. (Ed Osterwald)

Narrow gauge derrick OP in Alamosa yards, May 5, 1968. Note placement of grab irons, bracing on cab for A-frame, and supports on boom-tender flat car (06063) for the derrick boom and cables. (Ed Osterwald)

Flanger OL at Chama, 1973. Note the folding double blade. Flangers also have large chisels fitting inside the rails to clear away ice and hard-packed snow. The round red target (resembling a switch stand) tells the locomotive engineer whether the chisels are up or down; they must be raised when crossing switches. Blades and chisels are operated by air pressure from the locomotive. (C. R. Osterwald)

Front-quarter view of flanger OK at Chama, 1973, showing arch-bar trucks, shape of single flanger blade, hand-rail arrangement, brake cylinder on left end, and sheet-metal enclosure to protect the operating machinery. (C. R. Osterwald)

Water car W462 at Chama, 1972. These cars were used by the D&RGW to carry extra water for engines west of Chama. W462 was the tender of K-27 No. 462. (C. R. Osterwald)

Water car 0471 at Chama, 1972 after repainting for a display at Cumbres. This car carries extra water for rotary snowplow OM. (C. R. Osterwald)

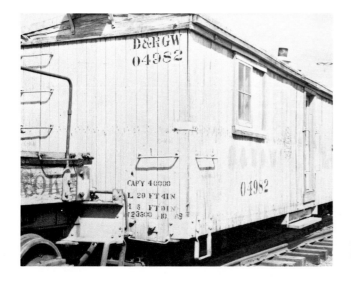

Outfit car 04982 at Chama, 1972. This car was used by the D&RGW as a rolling headquarters for section foremen. (C. R. Osterwald)

End detail of caboose 0503, showing roof walk supports, ladder assembly, and placement of retainer valve. Sept. 1972.

(Ed Osterwald)

C&TS caboose 0503 at Antonito, Oct. 3, 1970, had just been painted and lettered for the brand-new railroad by volunteer workers. Notice the different ladders on the left end, as compared to the ladder in the upper right picture on this page.

(D. B. Osterwald)

REFERENCES

HISTORY

Adams, Robert, 1974, The Architecture and Art of Early Hispanic Colorado: Colo. Assoc. University Press, in cooperation with The State Historical Society of Colo., 238 p.

Bauer, W. H., Ozment, J. L., and Willard, J. H., 1975, Colorado Postal History: The Post Offices: The Creete News, Inc., 248 p.

Brayer, Herbert O., 1949, William Blackmore: The Spanish-Mexican Land Grants of New Mexico and Colorado, 1863-1878, Vol. I: Bradford-Robinson Printing Co., Denver, 381 p.

Buchanan, Robert H., 1971, The San Luis Valley—A Land of Paradox, in New Mexico Geol. Soc. Guidebook, 22nd Field Conf., San Luis Basin, Colo., p. 243-245.

Catholic Church, Conejos, Colo., 1934, Articles on the parish churches in the Southern San Luis Valley: Antonito, Colo.

Crofutt, George A., 1885, Crofutt's Grip-Sack Guide of Colorado: CUBAR Reprint 1966, Golden, Colo., 264 p.

Daggett, Eleanor, 1973, Chama, New Mexico: Nature Trek Publication, Albuquerque, N. M., 22 p.

Dane, Carl H., 1960, Early Explorations of Rio Arriba County, N.M. and Adjacent Parts of Southern Colo., in New Mexico Geol. Soc. Guidebook, 11th. Field Conf., p. 113-127.

Flower, Judson Harold, Jr., 1966, Mormon Colonization in the San Luis Valley, 1878-1900, M.A. Thesis, Brigham Young Univ., 118 p.

Hill, C. C., 1949, Wagon Roads in Colo., 1858-1876, M.A. Thesis, Univ. of Colo.

Ingersoll, Ernest, 1885, The Crest of the Continent: R. R. Donnelley & Sons, Chicago, Ill., 344 p.

Lavender, David, 1954, Bent's Fort: Doubleday & Co., Garden City, N. Y., 450 p.

Pearce, T. M., editor, 1965, New Mexico Place Names, A Geographical Dictionary: Univ. of New Mexico, Albuquerque, N. M., 187 p.

Rivera, Art, 1973, Introducing Chama Country: La Chispa Promotions, Chama, N. M., 40 p.

Sarah Platt Decker Chapter, N.S.D.A.R., 1942, 1946, 1952, 1961, Pioneers of the San Juan Country: Vol. I and II, Outwest Printing Co., Vol. III, Durango Printing Co., Vol. IV, Big Mountain Press.

Sprague, Marshall, 1964, The Great Gates, the Story of the Rocky Mountain Passes: Little Brown & Co., Boston, Mass., 468 p.

State of Colorado Archives, Certificates of Incorporation for Toll and Wagon Roads in Colorado.

Stauter, Patrick C., 1958, 100 Years in Colorado's Oldest Parish: Ye Olde Print Shoppe, Alamosa, Colo., 40 p.

The San Luis Valley Historian: San Luis Valley Historical Society, Inc., Alamosa, Colo., Vol. I, No. 1, Jan. 1969, 15 p.

The San Luis Valley Historian: San Luis Valley Historical Society, Inc., Alamosa, Colo., Vol. I, No. 2, April 1969, 32 p.

The San Luis Valley Historian: San Luis Valley Historical Society, Inc., Alamosa, Colo., Vol. I, No. 3, July 1969, 36 p.

Ubbelohde, Carl, 1965, A Colorado History: Pruett Press, Inc., Boulder, Colo., 339 p.

U. S. Army Engineers, 1876, Annual Report of Chief of Engineers: (Ruffner Report) Wash., D.C.

U. S. Army Engineers, 1878, Report of the Chief of Engnieers: (Ruffner Report) Wash., D.C.

Valdez, Luis, and Steiner, Stan, editors, 1972, Aztlan, An Anthology of Mexican American Literature: Vintage Books, 410 p.

W.P.A. Writer's Program, 1948, Colorado, A Guide to the Highest State: Hastings House, N. Y., 511 p.

Westermeier, Clifford P., 1970, Colorado's First Portrait: Univ. of New Mexico Press, Albuquerque, N. M., 206 p.

Wheeler, G. M., 1889, Geographical Report: U. S. Geographical Surveys West of the 100th Meridian, Vol. I.

Wilson, Dorothy D., 1971, They Came to Hunt, Early Man in the San Luis Valley, in New Mexico Geol. Soc. Guidebook 22nd Field Conf., San Luis Basin, Colo., p. 203-207.

RAILROADS

Athearn, Robert G., 1958, The Independence of the Denver & Rio Grande; in Utah Historical Quarterly, Vol. XXVI, Jan. 1958. 21 p.

Athearn, Robert G., 1962, Rebel of the Rockies: Yale Univ. Press, New Haven, Conn., 395 p.

Best, Gerald M., 1968, Mexican Narrow Gauge: Howell-North Books, Berkeley, Calif., 180 p.

Beebe, Lucius, 1947, Mixed Train Daily: E. P. Dutton Co., New York, N. Y., 368 p.

Beebe, Lucius, 1958, Narrow Gauge in the Rockies: Howell-North Books, Berkeley, Calif., 224 p.

Beebe, Lucius, 1962, Rio Grande, Mainline of the Rockies: Howell-North Books, Berkeley, Calif., 380 p.

Brayer, Herbert O., 1949, William Blackmore: Early Financing of the Denver & Rio Grande Railway and Ancillary Land Companies, 1871-1878, Vol. II: Bradford-Robinson Printing Co., Denver, Colo., 333 p.

Chappell, Gordon, 1967, Farewell to Cumbres, in Colo. Railroad Museum, Rail Annual, 1967, p. 1-27.

Chappell, Gordon, 1969, To Santa Fe by Narrow Gauge, in Colo. Rail Annual, 1969, Colo. Railroad Museum, p. 3-47.

Chappell, Gordon S., 1971, Logging Along the Denver & Rio Grande: Colo. Railroad Museum, Golden, Colo., 190 p.

D&RG Railway Co., Timetable for 1890, reprinted by Colo. Railroad Museum, Golden, Colo.

Everett, George G., 1966, The Cavalcade of Railroads in Colo. from 1871 to 1965: Golden Bell Press, Denver, Colo., 235 p.

Gjevre, John A., 1971, Chili Line, the Narrow Gauge to Santa Fe: Rio Grande Sun Press, Espanola, N. M., 100 p.

Hauck, Cornelius W., and Richardson, Robert W., 1963, Steam in the Rockies, A Steam Locomotive Roster of the Denver & Rio Grande: Colo. Railroad Museum, Golden, Colo., 35 p.

Iron Horse News, compiled and edited by Robert W. Richardson for the Colo. Railroad Museum, Golden, Colo.

Le Massena, Robert A., 1974, Rio Grande to the Pacific: Sundance Ltd., Denver, Colo., 416 p.

Lind, Richard F., 1963, Narrow Gauge Country: Boulder, Colo., 132 p.

Maxwell, John W., Scale drawings of D&RGW equipment. Wheat Ridge, Colo.

Model Railroader Magazine, Apr. 1962, p. 47.

Myrick, David F., 1970, New Mexico's Railroads—An Historical Survey: Colo. Railroad Museum, Golden, Colo., 197 p.

Ormes, Robert M., 1963, Railroads and the Rockies: Sage Books, Denver, Colo. 406 p.

Thode, Jackson C., 1970, A Century of Passenger Trains, in The 1970 Denver Westerners Brand Book: Johnson Publishing Co., Boulder, Colo., p. 83-253.

GEOLOGY

Burroughs, R. L., and Butler, A. P., 1971, Rail Log Antonito, Colo. to Chama, N. M., in New Mexico Geol. Soc. Guidebook, 22nd Field Conf., San Luis Basin, Colo., p. 49-66.

Butler, Arthur P., 1971, Tertiary Volcanic Stratigraphy of the Eastern Tusas Mountains, Southwest of the San Luis Valley, Colo.-N.M., in New Mexico Geol. Soc. Guidebook, 22nd Field Conf., San Luis Basin, Colo., p. 289-300.

Chronic, John, and Chronic, Halka, 1972, Prairie Peak and Plateau, A Guide to the Geology of Colorado: Bull. 32, Colo. Geol. Survey, Denver, Colo., 126 p.

Geologic Atlas of the Rocky Mountain Region, 1972, Rocky Mountain Assoc. of Geol., 331 p.

Gray, M., McAfee, R., and Wolf, C. L., editors, 1972, Glossary of Geology: Am. Geol. Inst., Wash., D.C., 805 p.

James, H. L., 1971, Road Log No. 4, Chama, N.M. to Antonito, Colo. via Highway 17, in New Mexico Geol. Soc. Guidebook, 22nd Field Conf., San Luis Basin, Colo., p. 82-87.

Lipman, Peter W., 1969, Alkali and Tholeiitic Basaltic Volcanism Related to the Rio Grande Depression, Southern Colorado and Northern New Mexico, Geol. Soc. America Bull., Vol. 80, p. 1343-1353.

Lipman, Peter W., Steven, Thomas A., and Mehnert, Harald H., 1970, Volcanic History of The San Juan Mountains, Colorado, as indicated by Potassium-Argon Dating, Geol. Soc. America Bull. Vol. 81, p. 2329-2351.

Lipman, Peter W., 1975, Evolution of the Platoro Caldera complex and related rocks, Southeastern San Juan Mountains, Colo.: U.S.G.S. Prof. Paper 852, 128 p.

Lochman-Balk, C. and Bruning, J. E., 1971, Lexicon of Stratigraphic Names, in New Mexico Geol. Soc. Guidebook, 22nd Field Conf., San Luis Basin, Colo., p. 101-111.

Smith, Clay T., and Muehlberger, William R., 1960, Road Log from Taos to Chama to Cumbres Pass and return to Chama, in New Mexico Geol. Soc. Guidebook, 11th. Field Conf., p. 11-23.

Stokes, W. L., and Varnes, D. J., 1955, Glossary of Selected Geologic Terms, Colo. Sci. Soc. Proc. Vol. 16, 165 p.

NATURE

Arnberger, Leslie P., 1968, Flowers of the Southwest Mountains: Southwest Monuments Assoc., Globe, Ariz., 112 p.

Baerg, Harry J., 1955, How to Know the Western Trees: Wm. C. Brown Co., Dubuque, Iowa, 170 p.

Craighead, John J., Craighead, Frank C., Jr., and Davis, Ray T., 1963, A Field Guide to Rocky Mountain Wildflowers: Houghton Mifflin Co., Boston, Mass., 277 p.

Dixon, Hobart N., 1971, Flora of the San Luis Valley, in New Mexico Geol. Soc. Guidebook, 22nd Field Conf., San Luis Basin, Colo., p. 133-135.

Dodge, Natt N., 1967, 100 Roadside Wildflowers of Southwest Uplands: Southwest Monuments Assoc., Globe, Ariz., 32 p.

Hale, Mason E., 1969, How to Know the Lichens: Wm. C. Brown Co., Dubuque, Iowa, 226 p.

Harrington, H. D., 1964, Manual of the Plants of Colorado: Sage Books, Chicago, Ill., 666 p.

Jefferson County Schools, Activity File of Outdoor Education Laboratory Schools, 1976.

Keen, Veryl F., 1971, Fauna of the San Luis Valley, in New Mexico Geol. Soc. Guidebook, 22nd Field Conf., San Luis Basin, Colo., p. 137-139.

Kirk, Donald R., 1970, Wild Edible Plants of the Western United States: Naturegraph Publishers, Healdsburg, Calif., 307 p.

Nelson, Ruth Ashton, 1970, Plants of Rocky Mountain National Park: Rocky Mountain Nature Association & National Park Service, 168 p.

Patraw, Pauline M., 1964, Flowers of the Southwest Mesas: Southwestern Monuments Assoc., Globe, Ariz., 112 p.

Pesman, Walter M., 1967, Meet the Natives: 7th edition, Denver Botanic Gardens, 219 p.

Peterson, Roger Tory, 1961, A Field Guide to Western Birds: 2nd Ed., Houghton Mifflin Co., Boston, Mass., 309 p.

Sweet, Muriel, 1962, Common Edible and Useful Plants of the West: Naturegraph Co., Healdsburg, Calif., 64 p.

Weber, William A., 1967, Rocky Mountain Flora: Univ. of Colo. Press, Boulder, Colo. 437 p.

NEWSPAPERS AND MAGAZINES

Alamosa Expositor

Alamosa Independent Journal

San Luis Valley Courier — Alamosa

Valley Courier — Alamosa

Antonito Ledger

Antonito Ledger News

Colorado Springs Daily Gazette

Colorado Springs Weekly Gazette

Denver & Rio Grande Western Magazine, Vol. 2, No. 7, May 1926.

Durango Semi-Weekly Herald

The Green Light, D&RGW Employees Magazine, 1940 to present.

Silverton La Plata Miner

Silverton Standard and the Miner

Pagosa Springs News

Pueblo Daily Chieftan

Pueblo Weekly Colorado Chieftan

Rio Grande Sun Historical Edition, 1962. Espanola, N. M.

Santa Fe Daily New Mexican

Santa Fe Weekly New Mexican

SOURCES FOR GUIDE MAPS

Base maps were prepared from U. S. Geological Survey topographic maps.

The geologic maps were compiled from the following maps and supplemented with personal field work:

Burbank, W. S., Lovering, T. S., Goddard, E. N., Eckel, E. B., 1935, Geologic Map of Colo. U.S.G.S.

Burroughs, R. L., and Butler, A. P., 1971, Maps with Rail Log from Antonito, Colo., to Chama, N. M., in New Mexico Geol. Soc. Guidebook, 22nd Field Conf., San Luis Basin, Colo.

Dane, Carl H. and Bachman, George O., 1965, Geologic Map of New Mexico, U.S.G.S.

Lipman, Peter W., 1975, Geologic Map of the Lower Conejos River Canyon Area, Southeastern San Juan Mountains, Colo.: U.S.G.S. Map I-901.

Smith, Clay T., and Muehlberger, William R., 1960, Geologic Map of the Rio Chama Country, in New Mexico Geol. Soc. Guidebook, 11th Field Conf., Rio Chama Country.

Steven, T. A., Lipman, P. W., Hail, W. J., Barker, Fred, and Luedke, R. G., 1974, Geologic Map of the Durango Quadrangle, Southwestern Colo.: U.S.G.S. Map I-764.

U. S. Bureau of Land Management records on early surveys, southern Colorado and northern New Mexico.

Zack, the head brake-dog, in the man-house of engine 489 on a hot day in Chama.